NEW HEBRIDES

Postal rates, Postmarks,
Registration cachets / labels

NEW HEBRIDES
Postal rates, Postmarks, Registration cachets / labels

Malcolm H. Goyns and Roland Klinger

Published by Mahego

MAHEGO

Published by Mahego
BM Box 1349
London, WC1N 3XX
United Kingdom

All rights reserved. No part of this work may be reproduced or stored in an information retrieval system (other than for the purposes of review) without the express permission of the publisher in writing.

The rights of Malcolm H. Goyns and Roland Klinger to be identified as the authors of this work has been asserted by them in accordance with the Copyright, Designs and Patents Act 1988.

© **Copyright 2013: Malcolm H. Goyns & Roland Klinger**

British Library Cataloguing in Publication data
A catalogue record for this book is available from the British Library
ISBN 978-0-9926660-0-2

Printed and distributed for Mahego by Lightning Source

NOTE: The material contained in this book is set out in good faith for general guidance and no liability can be accepted for loss or expense incurred as a result of relying in particular circumstances made in this book. The laws and regulations are complex and liable to change, and readers should check the current position with the relevant authorities before making personal arrangements

CONTENTS

Section A – Postal rates

1.	Pre-Condominium era	3
2.	Classical Condominium era	17
3.	Modern Condominium era	45

Section B – Postmarks

4.	Regular postmarks (Type PM)	79
5.	Special postmarks (Type PS)	105
6.	Postage-paid marks (Type PP)	123

Section C – Registration cachets / labels (Type NR)

7.	Registration cachets / labels (1903-1950)	131
8.	Blue-frame registration labels (1949-1980)	141

Appendices

Appendix I. Printed-paper rates	155
Appendix II. Philatelic covers	157
Appendix III. Unauthorized postmarks (Type PU)	159
Appendix IV. Comparison with previous studies	167

Front cover illustration – Registered cover to France. The 1/3d (1fr50c) stamps were cancelled by the Vila Type PM7A postmark (dated 21st November 1928), which paid the 5d (50c) colonial letter rate and 10d (1fr) colonial registration fee. Registration is indicated by cachet NR6.

PREFACE

The island territory in the South Pacific currently known as the Republic of Vanuatu was, up until 1980, called the New Hebrides. The New Hebrides was a fascinating territory being neither a British, nor a French colony, but rather a joint colony that was under the dual control of these two colonial powers. It was a unique arrangement that was given the name, Condominium. As the territory was jointly administered by French authorities, and possibly because its postage stamps did not bear the image of the British monarch, many British colonial collectors have shunned the territory. Similarly, because British authorities jointly administered it, many French colonial collectors have avoided it. This has left the territory in something of a limbo with a relatively small group of supporters. This is a great pity, because the very nature of its Condominium status makes it both an eccentric and fascinating country to collect and research.

The lack of interest in the New Hebrides has meant that fundamental aspects of its postal history have remained little studied and are uncertain. In this book, we have attempted to redress this situation by analyzing the postal rates within the context of the evolution of its postal system. There are still aspects that need to be researched, particularly the airmails of the 1940s, but we believe this book offers a good basis for further studies. This analysis is focused on letter rates, postcards rates, air surcharges and registration fees, which are those that will interest most collectors. The postal rates section of the book has been developed from a series of articles that one us (MHG) published during 2012 in *Pacifica*, the journal of the Pacific Islands Study Circle of Great Britain (PISC). This book has allowed us to expand on those articles and to resolve certain questions. In addition, we are able to provide numerous illustrations of the different postal rates. This has been aided considerably by the archive of New Hebrides postal history that has been brought together in an award-winning website (www.ro-klinger.de/NH) by one of us (RK).

A major problem in studying New Hebrides postal history is the existence of a mass of incorrectly paid covers and postcards, which occur in all periods. These fall into two categories, namely incorrectly paid commercial mail and 'philatelic' covers. Mail from the first of these categories occurred because the sender may not have had the correct postage stamps, or may not have been sure of the postage required and therefore used whatever stamps they thought would cover the cost of the postage. This frequently occurred with ship mail, early airmails, but also postcards from the modern era. This type of mail is of interest as it reflects the underdeveloped nature of the postal service in the New Hebrides. The 'philatelic' covers have occurred throughout the history of the New Hebrides and were particularly prevalent from 1908 to 1926. We acknowledge that many collectors value such items. However, one of our hopes is that the information presented in this book will assist the purist in distinguishing genuine commercial mail from such ephemera.

One of the curiosities of New Hebrides postal history is the apparent scarcity of postcards showing the correct postage, during certain time periods. It appears postcards are much more common from the 1906-1912 and the 1972-1980 periods than from other times. In fact postcards are so scarce from the 1927-1938 period that we have never seen examples of some of the postal rates and that is despite the fact that together we have almost 60 years' experience of collecting New Hebrides postal history!

In this book, we also present a substantive revision of previous studies of New Hebrides postmarks and registration cachets / labels. There have previously been several significant listings, but the PISC listing of 1995 is the one that is generally recognized. Since 1995 we have gained considerably more knowledge concerning the postmarks. The use of computer technology has also allowed us to resolve a number issues and to redefine several of the postmark subtypes. This has resulted in a comprehensive revision of the subject.

Throughout our research and the subsequent development of this book we have received considerable help and encouragement from other New Hebrides collectors, who have provided both information and illustrations. In this regard, we would like to thank Jim Crompton (UK), John Gibson (Australia), Hubert Goron (Australia), Bill Holland (UK), Jacques Merot (France), Alain Millet (France), Sheryll Ruecker (USA), Serge Simonot (France) and Martin Treadwell (New Zealand).

Malcolm H. Goyns & Roland Klinger (2013)

The authors, Roland Klinger (left) and Malcolm Goyns (right) at the 50th anniversary meeting of the Pacific Islands Study Circle, which was held in June 2012 in York, England (Photo courtesy of the P.I.S.C.).

PACIFIC ISLANDS STUDY CIRCLE

The Pacific Islands Study Circle fosters the study of the philately and postal history of the smaller Pacific islands, plus Christmas and Cocos Islands in the Indian Ocean. We welcome new members, wherever they may live, and offer these services:

PACIFICA. Our magazine, size A4 and illustrated in colour, full of news items and articles about our area and activities, published four times a year and sent by airmail to overseas members. As an alternative to the printed version we offer a digital version which may be downloaded from our website at a substantially lower subscription rate – see below.

PUBLICATIONS. Research and reference publications are sold to members at cost price. There are over 20 titles in our current list, with another in preparation.
"MARKETPLACE". A facility for members to buy and sell surplus material via our website.
MEMBERS' FORUMS. Discussion groups for the islands which we cover, accessed via our website.
GROUP LEADERS, who can offer expert advice on their territories.
REGIONAL MEETINGS in the UK, and occasionally overseas.

The Study Circle is run by collectors for collectors. Dealers are most welcome to join if they belong to a recognized trade association. Payment for subscriptions, publications and auction purchases is accepted in a range of currencies and also by Paypal.

Subscriptions run from 1st January. Members joining after April will be sent all back issues for the current year or will be entitled to download them, depending on the type of membership chosen.

Membership application forms and current subscription rates may found on our web site (http://www.pisc.org.uk) or obtained from the Secretary (Email: info@pisc.org.uk).

New Hebrides Postal History

SECTION A

POSTAL RATES

Big Namba village in Malekula, New Hebrides. Postcard series (Unknown publisher), published circa 1906.

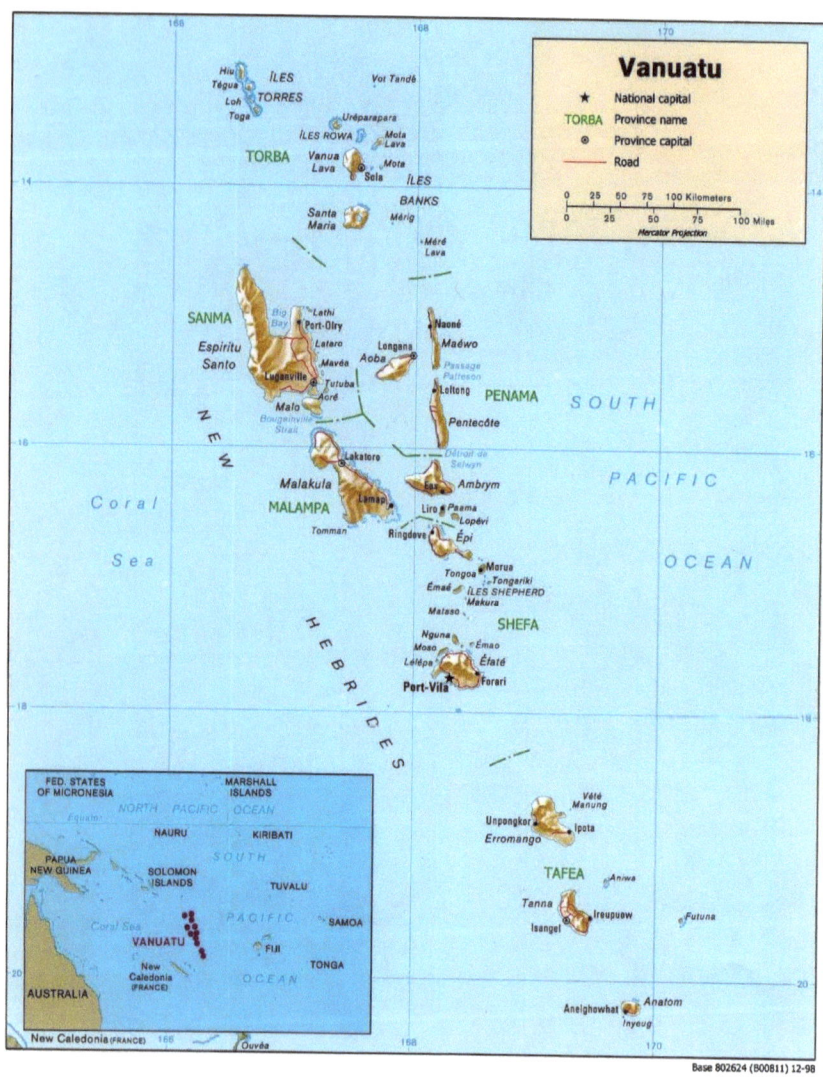

Map of the New Hebrides (Illustration courtesy of the University of Texas Libraries, The University of Texas at Austin).

1. PRE-CONDOMINIUM ERA (1891-1908)

Introduction

During the nineteenth century a small, but increasing, number of Europeans migrated to the New Hebrides. These were mainly missionaries, planters and traders. There was no postal service for most of this century and mail had to be carried by passing ships. Mail from the New Hebrides during this time can only be distinguished by an address written on the cover or letter (Figure 1). Much of this early mail was from missionaries, though a small number of covers are known that were written, or posted, on board passing ships.

Figure 1. Letter from the Samoan teacher Elia, who was based on Erromango in the New Hebrides, addressed to the missionary Henry Nisbet, Lalomalava, Savaii, Samoa. Inscription on letter reads, Eromaga 18th July 1855, Elia.

In 1888 the Australian United Steam Navigation Co (AUSNCo) was granted a subsidy by the authorities in Victoria to carry mail between Melbourne, the New Hebrides and Fiji. This was subsequently supplemented by a subsidy from the authorities in New South Wales (NSW), who decided to establish a postal agency in the New Hebrides. As the connecting point for interisland mail in the New Hebrides at that time was Aneityum, a part-time agent Mr. Martin, was appointed there on 1st August 1891. The following year saw a change in the shipping routes, so that mail was exchanged at Port Vila on Efate. The postal agency was therefore transferred to Efate and Mr. Le Couteur, who was the local AUSNCo representative, was appointed as the postal agent. The subsidies supporting this mail service were removed during the following year and the AUSNCo stopped its mail service in 1893. The mail service was then taken over by the Australian New Hebrides Co (ANHCo) whose local manager, Mr. Hood, became the unofficial postal agent in Port Vila. The NSW authorities subsidised this activity from 1894.

There were always tensions between the British and French settlers in these islands and the operation of the NSW postal agency resulted in agitation from French settlers for the establishment of a French postal agency. Eventually the New Caledonia (NC) postal authorities agreed to these demands. This NC postal agency began operating in 1903, but unlike the NSW agency, was ship-based. The two postal agencies operated in parallel and offered a postal service until the Condominium Post Office opened in 1908.

The operation of the NSW postal agency appears to have been an easy-going affair. Their postal rates were clearly based on those used in NSW, but changes in NSW rates were adopted only when it suited the agency. In contrast, the NC postal agency operated in a typically French bureaucratic manner and conscientiously applied charges in accordance with the prevailing French colonial postal rates. This perhaps explains why no official postal rates table has been found for the NSW agency, whose rates can only be inferred by studying postal history material, whereas the French colonial postal rates for this period are documented.

The agreement between Great Britain and France to establish a Condominium in the New Hebrides was finalised in 1906 and two years later the Condominium Post Office came into being. A 1908 proclamation from the British and French Resident Commissioners announced that the Condominium Post Office would issue the first New Hebrides provisional definitive stamps on 29th October 1908. This can, therefore, be regarded as the transition date between the ending of the Pre-Condominium era and the start of the classical Condominium era.

New South Wales Postal Agency

This agency used NSW stamps to pay the postage on mail that was sent to NSW and from there to the rest of the world. While the agency was based on Aneityum, a manuscript 'cross' was used to cancel the stamps. However, when the agency moved to Efate the following year, the Vila Type PM1 postmark was introduced to cancel the NSW stamps. The cost of postage on local mail, if any, is uncertain. As a subsidy was paid by the NSW authorities, it is probable that local mail was carried freely within the islands and that stamps were only required for mail to NSW and beyond. The postal rates used by the agency appear to have been based on those used in NSW (Table 1). These were a letter rate of 2½d per ½ ounce (Figure 2), a postcard rate of 1½d and a registration fee of 3d (Figure 3). These rates were applied irrespective of destination. We have never seen a postcard that was sent through the NSW agency prior to 1903 and therefore the suggested 1½d postcard rate cannot be confirmed and we are unable to illustrate it.

In the Hals & Collas book (details on page 167) it was stated that the NSW postal authorities reduced the charges for mail sent to British colonial destinations (including Great Britain) in 1899. Several writers have repeated this claim, but we can find no evidence for it. Our research into Australian newspaper archives leads us to conclude that the reduced letter rate of 2d was not introduced until 1st April 1905 and that the reduced 1d postcard rate not until 10th May 1905. This date for the new 2d letter rate is a better fit for the observed letter rates used by the NSW postal agency in Port Vila, which did not introduce the 2d rate until late in 1906 (or early 1907).

Studies of postcards sent through the NSW postal agency indicate that almost all were sent with the 1d rate from 1903. This corresponds with the establishment of the NC postal agency in 1903 (see below), which offered a 10c (1d) postcard rate. This commercial competition could explain why the NSW postal agency offered a 1d rate two years before the postal authorities in NSW reduced their rate. There was no similar competition to reduce the letter rate in 1903, because the NC agency rate for letters to non-French colonial destinations was 25c (2½d).

Figure 2. Cover to Canada. The 2½d NSW stamp, which was cancelled by the Vila Type PM1 postmark (dated 6th September 1897), paid the letter rate.

Figure 3. Registered cover to New South Wales. The 5½d NSW stamps, which were cancelled by a Type PM1 postmark (dated ?? January 1899 and back-stamped Sydney 19th January 1899), paid the 2½d letter rate plus 3d registration fee. The registration number (37) was added in manuscript.

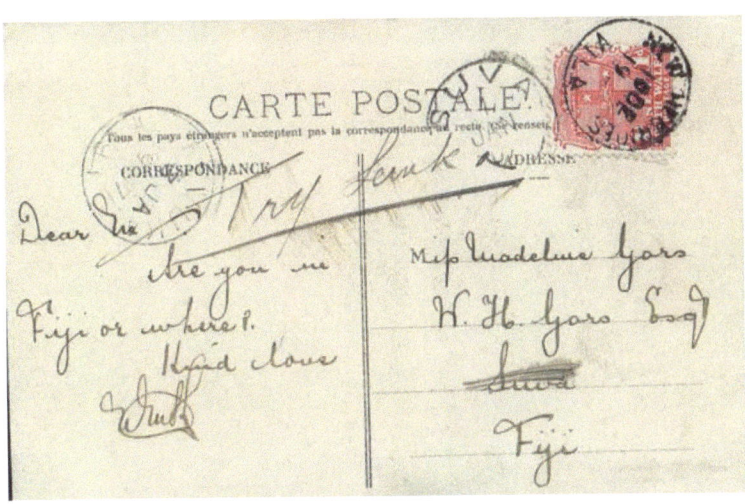

Figure 4. Postcard to Fiji. The 1d NSW stamp, which was cancelled by the Vila Type PM1 postmark (dated 10th December 1906), paid the postcard rate to British colonial destinations.

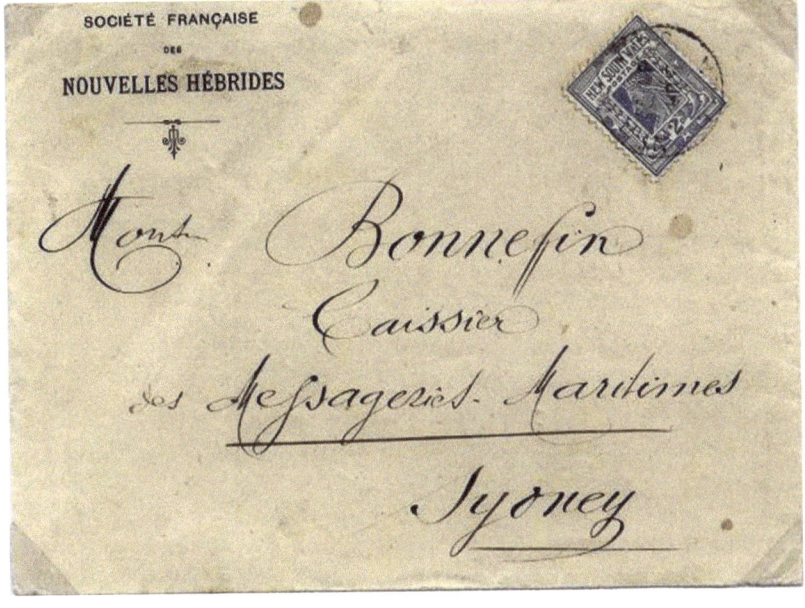

Figure 5. Cover to New South Wales. The 2d NSW stamp, which was cancelled by the Vila Type PM1 postmark (dated 15th April 1908), paid the letter rate to British colonial destinations that was introduced around 1906 / 1907.

Table 1. Postal rates used by the NSW postal agency (1891 – 1908)

Postal item		Charge
British colonial letter rate - per ½ oz (until 1906) (from 1906/07)		2½d 2d
All other destinations letter rate - per ½ oz		2½d
British colonial postcard rate (until 1903) (from 1903)		1½d ? 1d
All other destinations postcard rate		1½d ?
Registration fee	- All destinations	3d

In 1897 the ANHCo, whose ships carried mail throughout the islands and to NSW, introduced its own 'postage stamps' (1d, 2d). These were ostensibly for the payment of postage charges on local mail within the New Hebrides and also to pay a surcharge (in addition to the NSW stamps) on mail to NSW. The company had severe financial difficulties at the time and the proposal to supplement the postage on mail it transported (in addition to the annual £50 subsidy it already received) was probably a ruse for although 5,000 letters were posted annually, the ANHCo printed over 350,000 'postage stamps'. The intention was clearly to make money by selling these stamps to the philatelic trade and to achieve this, the ANHCo needed to have official approval for their use to enhance their 'postage stamps' status as being more than mere cinderellas. When the ANHCo approached the NSW postal authorities with their proposal, they were informed that the latter had no interest in postal affairs within the New Hebrides and would not sanction the use of the ANHCo 'postage stamps' on mail to NSW. The ANHCo subsequently released postal rates for interisland mail, which included a letter rate of 1d per ½oz and 2d registration fee. A few months after these 'postage stamps' went on sale, the ANHCo went out of business. Burns, Philip & Co Ltd (which was its parent company) appears to have assumed responsibility for the postal service and acquired the assets of the ANHCo, including their stocks of 'postage stamps', in September 1897. A few covers bearing ANHCo 'postage stamps' sporadically appeared (Figure 6), but the crucial fact is that most commercial mail to NSW was sent with only NSW stamps paying the postage. The status of the small number of covers bearing ANHCo 'postage stamps' posted between 1897-1900 is controversial. From 30th September 1900 a new agreement was signed between the NSW postal authorities and Burns, Philip & Co Ltd for the transport of mail, which included a formal ban on the use of ANHCo 'postage stamps'.

Figure 6. Cover to New South Wales. The 2½d NSW stamps, which were cancelled by the Vila Type PM1 postmark (dated 30th December 1897), paid the letter rate. The 1d and 2d ANHCo cinderellas were also cancelled by the same postmark, but were added for 'philatelic' reasons.

It appears that all reports claiming a genuine postal use for the ANHCo 'postage stamps' originated from the ANHCo, its parent company Burns Philip & Co Ltd., their employees, or Mr. Basset-Hull. The latter designed the ANHCo 'postage stamps' and was also editor of the *Australian Philatelist*, which published the articles that reported a genuine use for these 'postage stamps'. As this self-interested group of companies and individuals were responsible for all such reports and as there were no independent contemporary reports supporting their assertion, then one might reasonably conclude that these 'postage stamps' are cinderellas that had no genuine postal use.

New Caledonia Postal Agency

After years of lobbying by French settlers in the New Hebrides, the New Caledonia authorities established the NC postal agency in 1903 (20th March), which lasted until the opening of the Condominium Post Office in 1908. It appears that this was not land-based, but operated from ships of the Société Française des Nouvelles Hébrides or Messageries Maritimes. This offered a postal service using French colonial postal rates (Table 2) with New Caledonia stamps cancelled by either the Port Vila Type PM2, or the Port Sandwich Type PM3 postmark. The NC postal agency used metric weights unlike the imperial weights used by the NSW postal agency. These rates were divided between French colonial destinations (which included France) and other destinations. The letter rate to French colonial destinations was initially 15c (Figure 7), but was reduced to 10c in 1906 (Figure 8). The letter rate to all other destinations was 25c throughout this period (Figure 9), although there were changes in calculating the postage of overweight letters in 1907 (Table 2).

Figure 7. Cover to France. The 15c New Caledonia stamps, which were cancelled by the Port-Vila Type PM2 postmark (dated 28th May 1903), paid the letter rate to French colonial destinations until 1906.

New Hebrides Postal History

Figure 8. Cover to France. The 10c New Caledonia stamp, which was cancelled by the Port-Vila Type PM2 postmark (dated 15th March 1908), paid the French-colonial letter rate to French colonial destinations from 1906.

Figure 9. Cover to Fiji. The 25c New Caledonia stamps, which were cancelled by the Port-Vila Type PM2 postmark (dated 2nd December 1907), paid the letter rate to non-French colonial destinations.

The postcard rate was 10c (Figure 10), but a reduced rate of 5c was available for postcards with short messages (defined as not more than five words) posted to French colonial destinations. We have seen postcards with a 1c, 2c or 4c stamp cancelled with a NC agency postmark. It is probable that these cards were favour cancelled and then enclosed in a cover before being posted, which was a common practice at that time. One thing that is certain is that the reduced 5c postcard rate was the official French colonial rate from 1901 and throughout this period. Initially postcards with a short message sent to other destinations were charged at 10c, but in November 1905 this was also reduced to 5c (Figure 11).

The registration fee was 25c throughout this period, irrespective of destination (Figure 12).

Figure 10. Postcard to New Zealand. The 10c New Caledonia stamps, which were cancelled by the Port Sandwich Type PM3 postmark (dated ?? ?? 1907), paid the rate for postcards with a long message (more than five words). This rate was also applied to cards with a short message that were sent to non-French colonial destinations, prior to November 1905.

New Hebrides Postal History

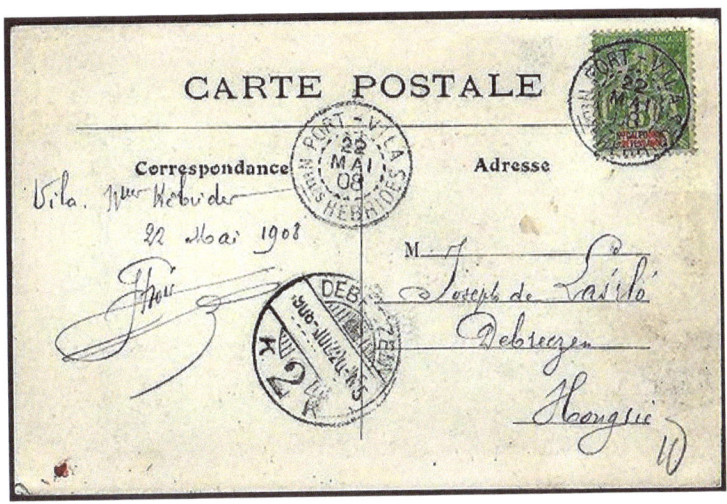

Figure 11. Postcard to Hungary. The 5c New Caledonia stamp, which was cancelled by the Port-Vila Type PM2 postmark (dated 22nd May 1908), paid the postcard rate for cards with a short message (not more than five words), which was applied to cards to French colonial destinations and, from November 1905, to other destinations.

Figure 12. Registered cover to France. The 35c New Caledonia stamps, which were cancelled by the Port Sandwich Type PM3 postmark (dated 25 September 1907), paid the 10c French colonial letter rate and 25c registration fee. Registration is indicated by cachet NR1B.

13

Table 2. Postal rates used by the NC postal agency (1903 – 1908)

Postal item		Charge
French colonial letter rate	- per 15g (until 15th April 1906) (from 16th April 1906)	15c 10c
All other destinations letter rate	- up to 15g (25c per extra 15g until 30th September 1907) (15c per extra 15g from 1st October 1907)	25c
French colonial postcard rate	- short message - long message	5c 10c
All other destinations postcard rate	- short message (until November 1905) (from November 1905)	10c 5c
All other destinations postcard rate	- long message	10c
Registration fee	- All destinations	25c

A group of covers is known cancelled by the NC postal agency Port Vila Type PM2 postmark, dated 23rd September 1903 and addressed to either Commandant Durafour or Captain Hervé in New Caledonia (Figure 13). These covers have a wide range of frankings, which can be confusing. However, none of the examples we have seen have New Caledonia backstamps and it appears they never passed through the post. These may have been postal service test covers produced by the U.C.N.C. as part of their attempt to take over the postal service contract from the Société Française des Nouvelles Hébrides. This would explain why so many of these covers have survived.

In September 1903, a group of local French entrepreneurs (including the notorious forger Mr. Alavoine) calling themselves the Syndicat Français des Nouvelles-Hébrides (SFNH) issued its own 'postage stamps'. It is probable that they chose this name so that they would be mistaken for the shipping company, Société Française des Nouvelles Hébrides. Although there is no evidence that this SFNH group was a genuine trading organization or even operated a shipping service, they claimed their 'postage stamps' would be used for a postal service. However, by the time they were issued the NC postal agency had come into operation and the SFNH 'postage stamps' were redundant. Irrespective of whether these were intended for a genuine postal service, or were simply a 'philatelic' moneymaking exercise, they had no postal validity. The SFNH series of four 'postage stamps' (5c, 15c, 25c, 1fr) were not recognised by any postal authority and should be regarded as cinderellas. The New Caledonia postal authorities banned their use and confiscated stocks within three weeks of their issue. Numerous covers are known bearing these cinderellas, which had been favour cancelled with a NC postal agency postmark. These are 'philatelic' concoctions that never passed through the post. If any of them did manage to pass through the post, they did so by accident and are little more than 'philatelic' curiosities. These cinderellas were also frequently attached to genuine mail sent through the NC postal agency (Figure 14). However, it is important to note that it was the New Caledonia stamps alone that paid the postage on that mail and the SFNH cinderellas were added only for 'philatelic' reasons.

Figure 13. UCNC postal service test cover addressed to Captain Hervé in New Caledonia. The 4c New Caledonia stamp, which was cancelled by the Port-Vila Type PM2 postmark (dated 23rd September 1903), paid the printed-paper rate (see Table 21).

Figure 14. Postcard (with a short message) to New Caledonia sent through the NC postal agency. The 5c New Caledonia stamp was cancelled by a Port Vila Type PM2 postmark (dated 23rd July 1908), which paid the French colonial postcard (short message) rate. The card also has a SFNH 5c cinderella. Although the latter was cancelled with the same postmark, it made no contribution to the payment of postage and was attached only for 'philatelic' purposes.

2. CLASSICAL CONDOMINIUM ERA (1908-1938)

Introduction

This section discusses postal rates used during the classical Condominium era, from the opening of the Condominium Post Office in 1908 (Figure 15) until the introduction of the 'virtual' gold currency in June 1938. It is important to remember that the New Hebrides was neither a British nor a French colony, but rather a British-French Condominium. As there was no precedent for administering such a territory, the Condominium officials had to develop their own procedures while being careful not to offend the sensibilities of either of the colonial powers. This was particularly true of the Condominium Post Office. The operation of a postal service created numerous opportunities for diplomatic disputes, as demonstrated by the French overprinting New Caledonia stamps without the word 'Condominium' in 1908, or the British printing French-language definitives on CA crown watermark paper in 1911. Furthermore, the parallel use of Australian, British and French currencies in the territory frequently created problems due to fluctuating currency exchange rates. The general confusion that appears to have pervaded the administration often resulted in the Condominium being referred to as the Pandemonium.

The Condominium Post Office was based in Port Vila, but several interisland vessels also collected mail from the outer islands and cancelled it with their own postmarks (see page 80). Throughout this era and into the modern era (with the exception of the British and French colonial rates of 1908-1920 and the local rates of 1927-1937), rates were divided between 'colonial' and 'non-colonial' destinations. The term 'colonial' is used here in its loosest sense to mean Great Britain, France and countries associated with them. These included British dominions, colonies, protectorates and mandated territories (from 1947 these would become British Commonwealth) and French colonies, protectorates and mandated territories. All other destinations are termed, 'non-colonial'.

We can find little official information regarding postal rates used before 1927, which may not exist because the rates had to be improvised by the Condominium Postmaster. The conclusions in Tables 3 and 4 are to a large extent based on studies of postal material. These studies were not straightforward as the period is awash with overpaid 'philatelic' covers. Studies of postal rates can be difficult with a territory such as the New

Hebrides when so much of the mail is incorrectly paid. From an analysis of over 700 covers, it is clear that at least 50% of covers from the 1908–1912, 1920–1921 and 1924-1926 periods exhibit incorrect postage. The percentage is even higher in the case of registered covers. This is mainly due to 'philatelic' activity associated with the issue of new definitive stamp series. Conversely, over 90% of postcards from the same periods show the correct postage.

Figure 15. The post office in Port Vila. Cliché Maison d'Art Colonial postcard series (number 11), published circa 1912.

The Condominium Post Office levied postage due charges on underpaid mail. This charge was double the underpaid amount. Initially the charge was indicated with a 'T' in triangle hand-stamp and the amount in manuscript (Figure 16). However in 1925, postage due stamps were introduced and used to indicate the charge on local or incoming underpaid mail (Figure 17).

Figure 16. Underpaid mail. 1909 cover to Germany paid with 20c stamps, but as the non-colonial letter rate was 25c, this was an underpayment of 5c. The postage due charge is indicated by a manuscript 0.10 (2x 5c).

Official mail from the administration offices did not require stamps. These covers bore the administration name and / or relevant acronym and were cancelled with a Port Vila postmark. The British administration used the inscription 'On His Majesty's Service' or O.H.M.S. acronym (Figure 18), the French administration used the inscription 'Residence de France' or S.O. (Service Officiel) acronym (Figure 19) and the Condominium administration, mostly the Post Office, used 'On Condominium Service' or O.C.S. acronym (Figure 20).

Figure 17. Underpaid cover from Indochina bearing only 10c Indochina stamps instead of the required 50c. The postage due charge is paid by 80c postage due stamps (2x 40c) cancelled by a Vila Type PM7B postmark (dated 25th November 1932).

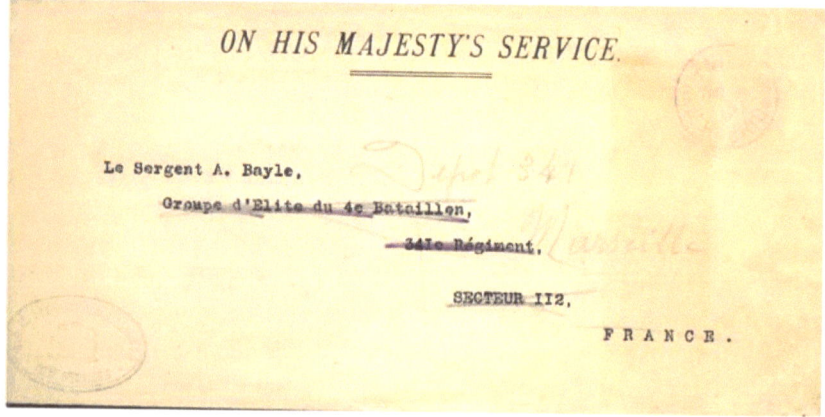

Figure 18. British administration cover to France, cancelled by Vila Type PM4 postmark (dated 8th November 1917).

Figure 19. French administration cover to France, cancelled by Port Vila Type PM6 postmark (dated 9 July 1931).

Figure 20. Condominium administration registered cover to Great Britain, cancelled by Vila Type PM7B postmark (dated 12th March 1937). Registration is indicated by cachet NR9.

1908-1920

The Condominium Post Office began operations on 29th October 1908 and its first set of postal rates lasted, with a few changes in 1912, until 31st August 1920 (Table 3). Given the political situation in 1908 it appears that the Condominium Postmaster developed a set of rates that reflected the rates from both of the postal agencies that had previously operated in the territory.

The letter rate to British colonial destinations was initially 2d (20c) per half ounce (Figure 21), but when in 1912 (December 10th) the New Hebrides joined the Empire Penny Post Scheme, this letter rate was reduced to 1d (10c) (Figure 22). We have seen comments that the New Hebrides may have joined the Empire Penny Post Scheme on 1st May 1911, but studies of covers to British colonial destinations clearly show a continued use of the 2d (20c) letter rate until December 1912. The letter rate to French colonial destinations was 10c (1d) per 15g throughout the period (Figure 23). The letter rate to non-colonial destinations was 2½d (25c), probably per 15g (Figure 24). It appears that local mail within the New Hebrides was treated as a French colonial destination.

It should be noted that Western Samoa was originally a German colony, but was annexed by New Zealand on 29th August 1914. Before that date, the Condominium Post Office regarded it as a non-colonial destination, but from that date it was regarded as a British colonial destination.

A universal postcard rate of 1d (10c) was adopted for all destinations (Figure 25). However, the reduced 5c (½d) rate for postcards with a short message was retained for cards sent to French colonial destinations (Figure 26).

The registration fee was 2½d (25c) throughout this period (Figure 27). Analysis of commercial registered covers indicates that prior to joining the Empire Penny Post Scheme in 1912, two registration fees may have existed in parallel with some mail paying the 25c fee and others a 2d fee. A 2d fee might have been adopted to minimise the difference between the British colonial and French colonial letter rates. When the British colonial letter rate was reduced in 1912, the 2d fee was no longer justified and was therefore abolished. This issue needs further investigation.

New Hebrides Postal History

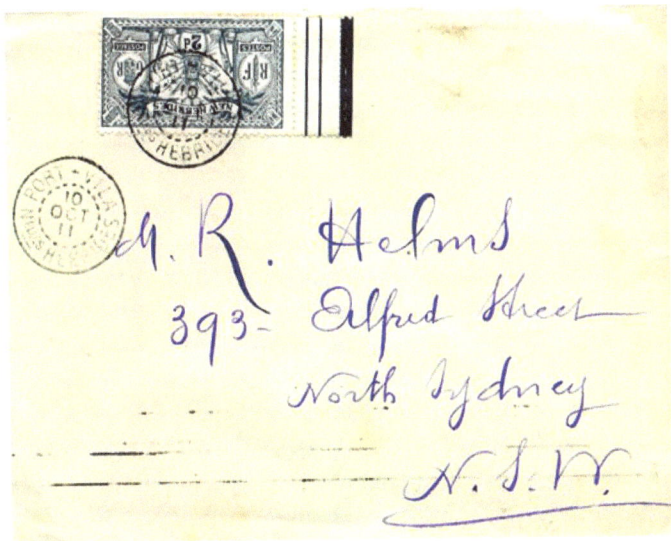

Figure 21. Cover to Australia. The 2d stamp, which was cancelled by the Port-Vila Type PM2 postmark (dated 10th October 1911), paid the British colonial letter rate until December 1912.

Figure 22. Cover to Malta. The 1d stamp, which was cancelled by the Port-Vila Type PM2 postmark (dated 22nd April 1915), paid British colonial letter rate after the New Hebrides joined the Empire Penny Post Scheme in 1912.

Figure 23. Cover to France. The 10c stamp, which was cancelled by the Service Maritime Type PM5A postmark (dated 29th December 1914), paid the French colonial letter rate.

Figure 24. Cover to the USA. The 2½d stamps, which were cancelled by the Port-Vila Type PM2 postmark (dated 12th June 1915), paid the non-colonial letter rate.

New Hebrides Postal History

Figure 25. Postcard to Switzerland. The 1d stamp, which was cancelled by the Port-Vila Type PM2 postmark (dated 27th March 1914), paid the postcard rate for cards to French colonial destinations with long messages and cards to all other destinations (irrespective of message length).

Figure 26. Postcard (with a short message) to New Caledonia. The 5c stamp, which was cancelled by the Port-Vila Type PM2 postmark (dated 20th November 1909), paid the (short message) postcard rate to French colonial destinations.

Figure 27. Registered cover to Sweden. The 3½d plus 15c stamps, which were cancelled by the Port-Vila Type PM2 postmark (dated 7th August 1911), paid the 25c (2½d) non-colonial letter rate and 25c (2½d) registration fee. Registration is indicated by cachet NR1C.

Figure 28. Registered cover to New Caledonia. The 5c New Caledonia stamp, 10c and 2d 1908 provisional definitives, which were cancelled by the Port-Vila Type PM2 postmark (dated 22nd November 1908), paid the 10c French colonial letter rate and 25c (2½d) registration fee. Registration is indicated by cachet NR1C.

It is worth noting that during the first month of its existence, the Condominium Post Office allowed the continued use of New Caledonia and NSW stamps, which were not officially banned until 1st December 1908 (Figure 28). Covers and postcards bearing these stamps are known after that date, but most appear to have been collected by S.S. Malaita from outer islands and cancelled with Type PM1. For example, a well-known group of postcards sent by Mr. Newman on Tongoa to Mr. Malmberg in New York had their postage paid by 1½d NSW stamps (which was by that time an overpayment) and dated 12th December 1908. The practice of accepting mail with NSW stamps continued into 1909 and the Condominium Post Office officials appear to have turned a blind eye to such mail landed at Port Vila by S.S. Malaita.

Table 3. Postal rates used by the Condominium Post Office (1908 – 1920)

Postal item		Charge
British colonial letter rate	- per ½ oz (until 9/12/1912) (from 10/12/1912)	2d (20c) 1d (10c)
French colonial letter rate	- per 15g	1d (10c)
Non-colonial letter rate	- per 15g	2½ d (25c)
British colonial postcard rate	- any message length	1d (10c)
French colonial postcard rate French colonial postcard rate	- short message - long message	½d (5c) 1d (10c)
Non-colonial postcard rate	- any message length	1d (10c)
Registration fee	- All destinations	2½d (25c)

1920-1927

New postal rates were introduced on 1st September 1920 and remained in force until 31st March 1927. This period has a relatively simple set of postal rates and yet there remains considerable debate about what were those rates. There are three reasons for this. First, confusion caused by the plethora of overpaid 'philatelic' mail produced mainly during 1920-1921 and 1924–1926. Second, confusion caused by debates of how unstable currency rates may have affected the value of stamps used on those covers. Third, confusion over whether the postal rates that had been proposed by the U.P.U. in 1924, were adopted by the Condominium Post Office. These confusions are discussed below, but here we deal with the actual rates, which are summarised in Table 4.

In 1920 the postal rates for mail to British and French colonial destinations were unified (this included local mail within the New Hebrides) and at the same time, metric weights were adopted for all mail. The colonial letter rate was 2d (20c) per 20g (Figure 29), with 1d (10c) increases for every extra 10g. The non-colonial letter rate was 3d (30c) per 20g (Figure 30), but differed in that overweight mail was calculated in multiples of 20g [3d (30c) per 20g]. It noteworthy that covers to non-colonial destinations showing the 3d (30c) postage rate are scarce, as almost all covers sent to these destinations during this period were 'philatelic' and registered.

The postcard rate to all destinations was 1d (10c) (Figure 31), but the ½d (5c) rate was retained for postcards with a short message that were sent to colonial destinations (Figure 32). During 1923 to 1924, a local entrepreneur appears to have manufactured a number of postcards (Unis France series), which had a favour-cancelled stamp (usually the 5c value) on the picture side (we have seen various dates). In this state, these 'philatelic' concoctions are not a problem. However, some purchasers of the cards clearly thought it amusing to write their name and address on them. The problem arises when non-colonial addresses were used, as it suggests that cards with no message could have been sent through the post to non-colonial destinations for ½d (5c), which is not true.

A single registration fee of 3d (30c) was adopted for all mail, irrespective of destination (Figure 33).

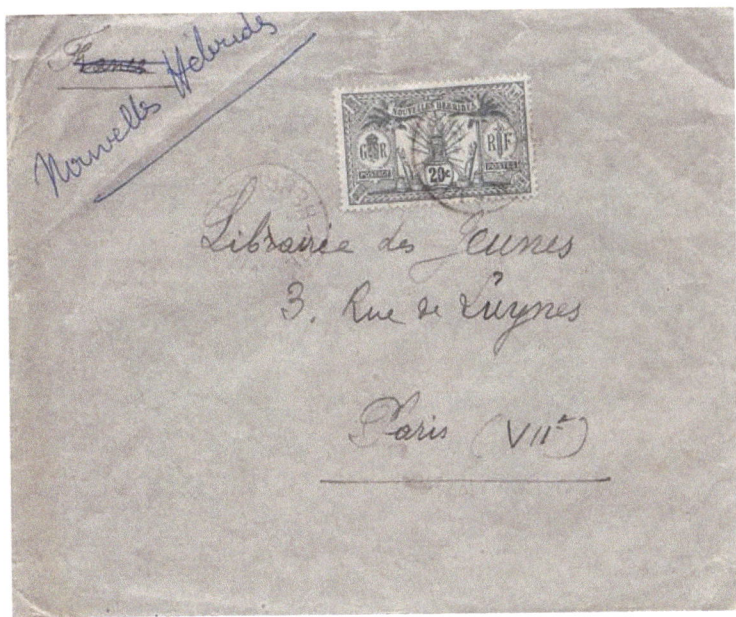

Figure 29. Cover to France. The 2d stamp, which was cancelled by the Vila Type PM4 postmark (dated 2nd January 1924), paid the colonial letter rate.

Figure 30. Cover to USA. The 1d plus 20c stamps, which were cancelled by the Vila Type PM4 postmark (dated 29th October 1920), paid the non-colonial letter rate.

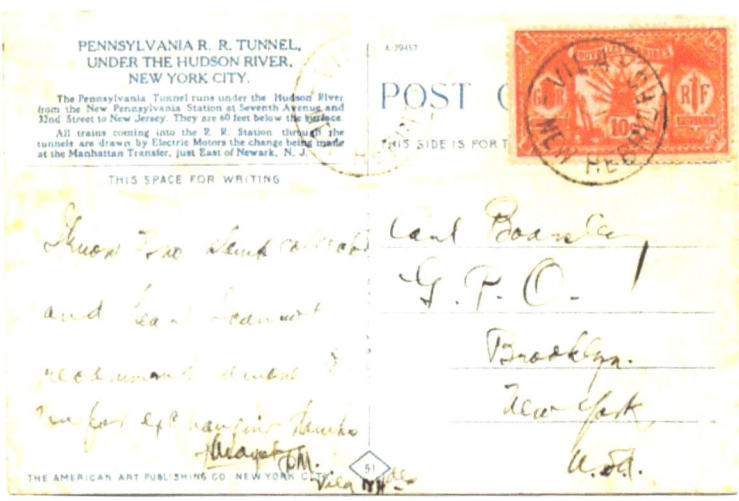

Figure 31. Postcard to USA. The 10c stamp, which was cancelled by the Vila Type PM4 postmark (dated 24th October 1924), paid the colonial (long message) and non-colonial postcard rates.

Figure 32. Postcard to France. The 5c stamp, which was cancelled by the Postes Condominium Type PM6 postmark (dated 2nd April 1925), paid the colonial (short message) postcard rate.

Figure 33. Registered cover to France. The 50c stamps, which were cancelled by the Service Condominium Type PM6 postmark (dated 16th July 1924), paid the 2d (20c) colonial letter rate and 3d (30c) registration fee. Registration is indicated by cachet NR3.

Table 4. Postal rates used by the Condominium Post Office (1920 – 1927)

Postal item		Charge
Colonial letter rate	- up to 20g - each additional 10g	2d (20c) 1d (10c)
Non-colonial letter rate	- up to 20g - each additional 20g	3d (30c) 3d (30c)
Colonial postcard rate	- short message - long message	½d (5c) 1d (10c)
Non-colonial postcard rate	- any message length	1d (10c)
Registration fee	- All destinations	3d (30c)

The release of several issues of definitive stamps in 1920-1921 and again in 1924-1925 stimulated philatelic activity. Numerous covers are known from these periods that show overpayment. The fact that postage on these covers is incorrect is indicated firstly by the wide variation in overpayment, secondly, by the existence of genuine commercial covers from the same period with their postage paid according to Table 4, and thirdly by the fact that many of these overpaid covers were sent to a small number of addressees (see Appendix II). As these covers are 'philatelic' it is unnecessary to explain their overpayment in terms of fluctuating currency exchange rates. In fact, such an approach would have to be applied to all covers posted at the same time and given the wide variation in overpayment and the presence of genuine commercial covers, such an approach becomes meaningless. It is of course possible that the amount charged at the counter may have been greater than the value printed on the stamp, but the crucial fact is that the value of the stamps on commercial covers was constant throughout this period.

In 1924 the U.P.U. proposed that the postcard rate be paid with a 1d (10c) green stamp, local letter rate by a 3d (30c) red stamp and overseas letter rate by a 5d (50c) blue stamp. This resulted in the Condominium Post Office issuing a short series of provisional overprints in line with the U.P.U. proposal. However, there is little evidence that these rates were ever adopted. The 1d (10c) postcard rate was already the normal rate and the use of the reduced ½d (5c) rate continued after 1924. There is no evidence for a 3d (30c) local letter rate at any time. The 5d (50c) for overseas letters was introduced in 1927, but only for colonial destinations, with the non-colonial letter rate being 1/3d (1f 50c).

1927-1937

New postal rates were introduced on 1st April 1927 and remained in force until 31st December 1937. These represented a major reorganization of the rates and included the separation of mail posted within the New Hebrides into a new local mail category. There were therefore three categories of postal rates i.e. local, colonial and non-colonial. Each of these categories had their own letter, postcard and registration rates (Table 5).

The letter rates (up to 20g) for local, colonial and non-colonial destinations were 2d (20c), 5d (50c) and 1/3d (1fr 50c) respectively (Figures 34-36). The postage for overweight letters was calculated in varying ways (see Table 5). We have noted some covers sent to local addresses within the New Hebrides with 1d (10c) postage, which would have contained printed-papers, as the local printed-paper rate was 1d (10c) per 50g. Similarly, a group of covers to the U.S.A. (dated 5th November 1934) with 3d (30c) postage are known. These apparently contained a printed description of New Guinea, which was regarded as printed-paper. The printed-paper rate to non-colonial destinations was 3d (30c) per 50g (see Appendix I).

The postcard rates were even more complex. The local and colonial rates for cards with long messages were 2d (20c) and 4d (40c) respectively, whereas cards with short messages were 1d (10c) and 2½d (25c) respectively. A new innovation was a colonial rate for a postcard with no message at 1½d (15c). The non-colonial postcard rate was 9d (90c) irrespective of message length. It should be noted that postcards, which show the correct postage, are scarce during this period. We have never seen one posted to a local address. We illustrate the colonial no message rate (Figure 98, see page 170), short message rate and long message rate as well as the non-colonial rate (Figures 37-39).

Different registration fees were introduced for local [4d (40c)], colonial [10d (1fr)] and non-colonial [1/3d (1fr 50c)] mail. This meant that the costs of sending a registered letter to local, colonial or non-colonial destinations were 6d (60c), 1/3d (1fr 50c) or 2/6d (3fr) respectively. We have never seen an example of the local registration fee. The colonial registration fee and non-colonial registration fee are illustrated in Figures 40 and 41 respectively.

Figure 34. Cover to Malakula. The 2d stamp, which was cancelled by the Vila Type PM7B postmark (dated 11th July 1936), paid the local letter rate.

Figure 35. Cover to France. The 5d (50c) stamps, which were cancelled by the Vila Type PM7B postmark (dated 25th February 1935), paid the colonial letter rate.

Figure 36. Cover to USA. The 1/3d (1fr 50c) stamps, which were cancelled by the Vila Type PM7B postmark (dated 6th September 1934), paid the non-colonial letter rate.

Figure 37. Postcard to France. The 2½d (25c) stamp, which was cancelled by the Postes Condominium Type PM6 postmark (dated 8th September 1927), paid the colonial (short message) postcard rate.

Figure 38. Postcard to France. The 4d (40c) stamps, which were cancelled by the Vila Type PM7B postmark (dated 11th August 1933), paid the colonial (long message) postcard rate.

Figure 39. Postcard to Switzerland. The 9d (90c) stamps, which were cancelled by the Vila Type PM7B postmark (dated 24th October 1933), paid the non-colonial postcard rate.

Table 5. Postal rates used by the Condominium Post Office (1927 – 1937)

Postal item		Charge
Local letter rate	- up to 20g - each additional 20g	2d (20c) 1d (10c)
Colonial letter rate	- up to 20g - up to 50g - up to 100g	5d (50c) 7½d (75c) 10d (1fr)
Non-colonial letter rate	- up to 20g - each additional 20g	1/3d (1fr 50c) 9d (90c)
Local postcard rate	- short message - long message	1d (10c) 2d (20c)
Colonial postcard rate	- no message - short message - long message	1½d (15c) 2½d (25c) 4d (40c)
Non-colonial postcard rate	- any message length	9d (90c)
Registration fee	- Local	4d (40c)
	- Colonial	10d (1fr)
	- Non-colonial	1/3d (1fr 50c)

The 1920s and 1930s saw a worldwide expansion of airmail, though the Condominium Post Office was, as usual, slow to adopt this new service. Occasional overpaid covers are known from the late 1920s to 1934, which were attempts to send letters by airmail for at least part of their journey. These were opportunistic and do not represent an official service. A series of covers are also known dated 16th July 1929, which commemorated a visit to the Pacific region by the French cruiser S.S. Tourville. This ship carried a seaplane that could transfer mail to and from nearby ports. The Condominium Postmaster had been alerted to this opportunity and therefore had a PAR AVION hand-stamp prepared, which was applied to each stamp on the mail to be collected by the seaplane. There is doubt as to whether this mail (thought to number 800 items) was ever flown to Noumea, because of problems with the seaplane, and it may actually have been shipped to Noumea by S.S. Tourville, after which it continued its journey in the normal manner. A small number of commercial covers with their postage paid according to the usual surface rate (Table 5) were included in this post, but most were grossly overpaid items (Figure 42). There was no obvious official surcharge for using this service, which was simply an opportunity for stamp collectors / dealers to exercise their 'philatelic' fantasies.

Table 6. Air letter rates from Sydney (1935 – 1938)

Destination	Air letter rate (per ½ oz)	Air postcard rate
Australia (internal)	3d	?
New Zealand	7d	?
Ceylon, India	1/2d	7d
Brunei, North Borneo, Sarawak, Singapore, Hong Kong	9d	5d
Indo-China, Japan, Philippines	10d	5d
Africa	1/6d	10d
Middle East	1/6d	9d
Great Britain	1/6d	9d
Europe (including France)	1/9d	9d
Canada	1/6d	?
U.S.A.	1/7d	?

It was not until the end of 1934 that a regular service was agreed. This service appears to have started early in 1935 and involved shipping mail to Sydney and then flying it from there to its destination. An airmail inscription on the front and a Sydney Air back-stamp can readily identify these covers (Figure 43). The postage charge was calculated by adding the appropriate surface mail rate (plus a registration fee if required) to the relevant air letter rate from Sydney. The air letter rates for the most common destinations are listed in Table 6. We also list most of the air postcard rates, but we have never seen an example of a postcard sent from the New Hebrides by airmail during this period. As the surface rate was calculated in metric weight and the air letter rate in imperial weight, this appears to have caused considerable confusion. As a result, almost all of these airmail covers show incorrect (overpaid) postage.

Figure 40. Registered cover to France. The 1/3d (1fr 50c) stamps, which were cancelled by the Interisland Service Type PM8 postmark (dated 25th July 1937), paid the 5d (50c) colonial letter rate and 10d (1fr) colonial registration fee. Registration is indicated by cachet NR11B.

Figure 41. Registered cover to Austria. The 2/6d (3fr) stamps, which were cancelled by the Vila Type PM7A postmark (dated 5th March 1929), paid the 1/3d (1fr 50c) non-colonial letter rate and 1/3d (1fr50c) non-colonial registration fee. Registration is indicated by cachet NR6.

Figure 42. Tourville cover to New Caledonia. The 4fr 95c stamps, which were cancelled by a Vila Type PM7A postmark (dated 16th July 1929), represented an overpayment of 3fr 45c. There is a manuscript 'R' and number (864) that might indicate the cover was registered. Even if this was the case, the postage is still overpaid. Note that the PAR AVION hand stamp has an oval '0' and not the round 'O' found in faked examples.

Opposite - Figure 43. Airmail cover to France. This cover, which has an airmail inscription on the front, was posted on board the interisland vessel S.S. Morinda, with the 5/- (6fr 25c) stamp cancelled by the Inter-island Type PM9A postmark (dated 4th July 1936). This overpaid the postage by 2/10d (3fr 40c). The cover would have been landed in Efate where a Port-Vila Type PM11A postmark (dated 8th July 1936) was applied, before it was shipped to Australia and from there flown to France. There is a Sydney Air transit mark (dated 15th July 1936) and a Paris arrival mark (dated 30th July 1936) on the back.

New Hebrides Postal History

1938 (January – May)

The introduction of the gold currency and the issue of the new gold currency definitive stamp series on 1st June 1938 brought to an end the classical Condominium era and began the modern Condominium era. There were new postal rates adopted for this new currency, which represented a general increase in charges. As the exchange rate for the new currency was initially 1 to 6 this meant, for example, that the new colonial letter rate of 10gc was effectively an increase from 5d (50c) to 6d (60c).

Analysis of postal material from 1938 indicates that these new rates were actually introduced some months before the issue of the gold currency stamp series. The earliest cover we have seen with the new rate was postmarked 26th January and as changes in surface postal rates usually occurred on the first day of the month, it is reasonable to conclude the new rates (in Australian / French currency) were introduced on 1st January 1938. These rates are summarised in Table 7 and lasted until 31st May, after which they were replaced by equivalent rates in gold currency.

The new postal rates abolished the previous local rate category that had been introduced in 1927 and local mail was again included with the colonial rates. The colonial and non-colonial letter rates were 6d (60c) and 1/6d (1f 80c) respectively. A single colonial postcard rate (irrespective of message length) was introduced, which was 6d (60c). The non-colonial postcard rate was 1/- (1f 20c). The registration fees were 1/- (1f 20c) for colonial destinations and 1/6d (1f 80c) for non-colonial destinations. Throughout the classical Condominium era, genuine commercial mail to non-colonial destinations was far scarcer than mail to colonial destinations. The majority of covers sent to non-colonial destinations during this time were 'philatelic' and mainly a response to new stamp issues. It is therefore unsurprising that we have not seen any examples of mail sent to non-colonial destinations during the short January – May 1938 period and are only able to illustrate examples of mail to colonial destinations (Figures 44 and 45).

Airmail continued to be shipped to Sydney, before being flown to its destination. The postage was the surface rate (Table 7) plus the airletter rate from Sydney (Table 6). However, overpayment of these air covers was still the norm (Figure 46).

New Hebrides Postal History

Figure 44. Cover to New Caledonia. The 6d (60c) stamp, which was cancelled by the Vila Type PM7B postmark (dated 6th April 1938), paid the colonial letter rate.

Figure 45. Registered cover sent to France. The 1/6d (1fr 80c) stamps, which were cancelled by the Vila Type PM7B postmark (dated 30th March 1938), paid the 6d colonial letter rate and 1/- colonial registration fee. Registration is indicated by label NR10B.

Table 7. Postal rates used by the Condominium Post Office (January – May 1938)

Postal item		Charge
Colonial letter rate	- per 20g	6d (60c)
Non-colonial letter rate	- per 20g - each additional 20g	1/6d (1f 80c) 1/- (1f 20c)
Colonial postcard rate		6d (60c)
Non-colonial postcard rate		1/- (1f 20c)
Registration fee	- Colonial	1/- (1fr 20c)
	- Non-colonial	1/6d (1f 80c)

Figure 46. Registered airmail cover to France. The 5/10d (7fr25c) stamps, which were cancelled by the Vila Type PM7B postmark (dated 27th May 1938), overpaid the postage by 2/7d. Registration is indicated by cachet NR9.

3. MODERN CONDOMINIUM ERA (1938-1980)

Introduction

This section discusses postal rates used during the modern Condominium era, from the introduction of the 'virtual' gold currency in 1938 until Independence and the emergence of the Republic of Vanuatu in 1980. This era witnessed an increasing amount of mail sent by air, even within the New Hebrides. Though in the latter case the airmail was only charged the surface mail rate. New post offices were also opened throughout the territory. These were Santo (1940-), Forari (1962-1969), Lamap (1962-1978), Tanna (1963-), Longana / Lolowai (1970-), Melsisi (1972-1978), Norsup (1975-) and Tongoa (1976-). Shipboard cancels continued to be carried by interisland vessels until the 1940s (see page 80).

The introduction of the gold currency on 1st June 1938 required that a new set of postal rates be adopted. This 'virtual' currency was needed to provide a standard whereby the cost of buying a stamp using either Australian or French colonial currency could be easily calculated despite fluctuating currency exchange rates. The gold currency consisted of 100 gold centimes (gc) to one gold franc (gf) and the exchange rates in June 1938 were 10gc to 6d or 60c (Australian or French currencies respectively). Within a year the British and French Resident Commissioners decreed that the gold currency exchange rate should be linked to the prevailing French colonial postal rates. This produced a confusing situation with the gold currency exchange rate changing to 1gf to 9fr in 1939, then 1gf to 10fr in 1940. We have seen letters from the Condominium Postmaster in which the exchange rate is stated to be 1gf to 15fr (dated 20th May 1943) and 1gf to 16fr (dated 12th April 1946). The latter also stated the Australian currency exchange rate was 1gf to 2/-. This issue clearly needs further study.

The 1925 definitive stamp series was not demonetized and therefore mail is known throughout the 1940s and later, which had its postage paid by these stamps. The Condominium Post Office no longer sold the 1925 stamps and their value in gold currency was related to the 1938 exchange rate. That is, a 6d / 60c stamp from the 1925 series would pay the colonial letter rate instead of a 10gc stamp.

Throughout this era, until 1977 when a comprehensive change occurred, the postal rates continued to be divided between colonial and non-colonial destinations (for definition of 'colonial' see page 17). Most of the postal rates are fairly straightforward as many rate tables are published, but the situation concerning airmail surcharges used up to 1953 is complex and the description given here needs further development.

The postage due charge continued to be double the underpaid amount (Figure 47). It should be noted that the use of postage due stamps was gradually phased out from the early 1960s as stocks were depleted. The Condominium post offices subsequently indicated the postage due charge in manuscript. The larger post offices used up their postage due stamp stocks during the 1960s, but smaller post offices were still using them into the 1970s.

Figure 47. Unstamped cover from France to the New Hebrides. The cover has no French stamps and only an Assignan postmark (dated 26th July 1971). The colonial letter rate was 20gc and therefore the postage due charge was 2x 20gc, which was paid by the 40gc postage due stamps, cancelled by a Longana postmark Type PM36B postmark (dated 18th August 1971).

Prior to 1952 a number of covers exist that bear much greater values of postage due stamps than would be warranted by a double-the-underpaid-amount charge. Closer analysis of these covers leads us to conclude that they are 'philatelic'. The most blatant of these is a group of covers addressed to Mr. L.I. Schreiber in 1951, which had various combinations of postage due stamps. These covers were probably favour-cancelled by the Condominium Post Office and several appear to have faked 'T' postage due hand-stamps. As such, these are 'philatelic' concoctions of little significance.

Official mail from the British, French and Condominium administrations increasingly used stamps from the 1940s. The availability of airmail during this decade meant that official mail could be flown to overseas destinations and stamps were initially required to pay the air surcharge. When the second-class airmail service was introduced in 1953, official airmail to overseas destinations could be sent stampless by second-class airmail and stamps were only needed to pay the air surcharge on mail sent by first-class airmail. The situation became more complex during the 1960s when mail to overseas destinations had the full postage (letter rate, registration fee, air surcharge) paid with stamps (Figure 48), or in the late 1970s by postage-paid marks. Although airmail became the norm for sending post within the New Hebrides during the 1960s, all official mail continued to be stampless when sent within the territory (Figure 49). This mail was identified by an appropriate Administration Department cachet, which was applied to the front of the cover. The only exception to this was mail from the Condominium Post Office, which sometimes only had the O.C.S. acronym, but no Service Des Postes cachet.

The situation for overseas mail from the Condominium Post Office was more complex. In the late 1960s, postage-paid marks were introduced so that stamps were not required (unlike overseas post from the British, French and other Condominium Administration offices). After this time and throughout the 1970s mail from the Condominium Post Office is found either with postage-paid marks plus the Service Des Postes cachet (Figure 50) or with stamps but no cachet (Figure 51). Anecdotal evidence indicates that although the Condominium Post Office routinely used postage-paid marks during this period, the officials were prepared to affix stamps to covers at the request of collectors. As long as the value of the stamps used on this mail covered the required postage charge, no objection was made to overpayment, which frequently occurred.

Figure 48. OHMS airmail cover to Great Britain. The 60gc stamps were cancelled by the Vila Type PM30A postmark (dated 2nd March 1965), which paid the 10gc colonial letter rate plus 50gc (up to 5g) UK air surcharge.

Figure 49. OCS cover to Port Vila. The cover is stampless (despite being flown within the New Hebrides) and cancelled by a Santo Type PM28B postmark (dated 31st December 1975). The cachet indicates the originating Condominium Administration Department was the Santo customs.

New Hebrides Postal History

Figure 50. OCS airmail cover from the Condominium Post Office to the USA. The use of a Vila postage paid-mark Type PP2C (dated 6th September 1976) meant that stamps were not needed.

Figure 51. OCS airmail cover from the Condominium Post Office to New Zealand. The 65gc stamps were cancelled by the Vila Type PM30B postmark (dated 9th April 1976), which paid the 25gc colonial letter rate plus 40gc (20g first class) New Zealand air surcharge.

49

1938-1960

Although there were some changes to the surface postal rates in 1949 and 1950, it is useful to regard 1938 (1st June) to 1960 (31st December) as a single period. This is because the colonial letter rate remained constant, as did the registration fees for both colonial and non-colonial destinations. The colonial letter rate was 10gc per 20g (Figure 52) with a postcard rate of 10gc. On 1st July 1950 the postcard rate was reduced to 5gc and there were also changes to the charges for overweight mail. The colonial registration fee was 20gc (Figure 53) throughout this period (Table 8).

Initially, the non-colonial letter rate was 30gc [up to 20g] (Figure 54) with a postcard rate of 20gc. These rates were reduced to 20gc (Figure 55) and 10gc respectively on 23rd August 1949, which also saw changes to the charges for overweight letters. The non-colonial registration fee was 30gc (Figure 56) throughout the period (Table 8). We have also noted numerous covers sent to the USA during the early 1940s with the postage paying only the 10gc colonial letter rate. This was not a consistent event and could have been a genuine mistake on the part of American service personnel, which given the wartime circumstances the Condominium Postmaster chose to ignore.

The surface postal rates were relatively straightforward during this period, but the same cannot be said of the airmail surcharges. Throughout the first decade the situation was complex with several flight routes, some of which operated for relatively short periods. Generally, airmail was shipped or flown to Sydney and from there flown to the rest of the world. There were also times when airmail was sent via Noumea or Auckland to its destination. The air surcharge tables presented here show the charges to the most common destinations. Despite improvements in the postal service during this era, incorrectly paid airmail covers and postcards were still common.

Up to 1945 the air surcharges are listed in Australian or French currency (Tables 9 and 10). It appears that 1gf may have been equivalent to 2/- (Australian) for the latter part of this period. From the limited number of airmail covers we have been able to analyze, it appears that the air surcharge to France (probably per 5g) was 1gf 20gc up to June 1939 (Figure 57), 80gc from July to December 1940 and 75gc from January 1940. This area needs further investigation

Figure 52. Cover to Great Britain. The 10gc stamp was cancelled by a Vila Type PM18A postmark (dated 2nd September 1953), which paid the colonial letter rate.

Figure 53. Registered cover to New Zealand. The 30gc stamps were cancelled by a Port-Vila Type PM11A postmark (dated 20th May 1941), which paid the 10gc colonial letter rate plus 20gc colonial registration fee. Registration is indicated by label NR10C.

Figure 54. Cover to USA. The 30gc stamps were cancelled by Vila Type PM7C and Port-Vila Type PM11A postmarks (dated 13th January 1942), which paid the 1938-1949 non-colonial letter rate.

Figure 55. Cover to Bulgaria. The 20gc stamps were cancelled by a Vila Type PM18A postmark (dated 2nd March 1957), which paid the 1949-1960 non-colonial letter rate.

Figure 56. Registered cover to USA. The 60gc stamps were cancelled by a Port-Vila Type PM11A postmark (dated 12th July 1944), which paid the 1938-1949 non-colonial letter rate, plus the 30gc non-colonial registration fee. Registration is indicated by cachet NR9.

Initially airmail was shipped to Sydney before being flown to its destination, but within a few months an all-up service (via Sydney) was introduced. The latter was part of the Empire Air Mail Scheme, with the inaugural flight arriving in Port Vila on 23rd September 1938. This service lasted until the outbreak of war with the last flight departing Sydney for Great Britain on 24th August 1939. A wartime service began the following month with the first flight leaving Sydney for Great Britain on 6th September 1939. As far as we can tell, mail from the New Hebrides at this time reverted to being shipped to Sydney before being flown to its destination. An all-up service was reintroduced in 1942, with the inaugural flight from Sydney arriving in Port Vila on 10th August. It is unclear how long this all-up service lasted, as it appears that by 1945 airmail was again being shipped to and from Sydney. Throughout this period it appears that airmail postage from the New Hebrides was calculated by adding the surface rate (Table 8) to the air rates from Sydney (Table 9). The only variation occurred during the Empire Air Mail Scheme period when the airmail rate to Great Britain (and British colonial destinations) from Australia was reduced.

Table 8. Surface postal rates used by the Condominium Post Office (1938 – 1960)

Postal item		Charge
Colonial letter rate (until 1950)	- per 20g	10gc
Colonial letter rate (from 1950)	- up to 20g	10gc
	- up to 50g	20gc
	- up to 100g	30gc
Non-colonial letter rate (until 1949)	- per 20g	30gc
	- each additional 20g	20gc
Non-colonial letter rate (from 1949)	- per 20gc	20gc
	- each additional 20g	10gc
Colonial postcard rate	(until 1950)	10gc
	(from 1950)	5gc
Non-colonial postcard rate	(until 1949)	20gc
	(from 1949)	10gc
Registration fee	- Colonial	20gc
	- Non-colonial	30gc

Figure 57. Air cover to France. The 1gf 30gc stamps were cancelled by a Vila Type PM7B postmark (dated 19th January 1939), which paid the 10gc colonial letter rate, plus the 1gf 20gc (up to 5g) France air surcharge.

In 1940 an additional air service began (Pan American Trans-Pacific Air Service) with the inaugural flight arriving in Auckland on 17th July. This transported mail from San Francisco across the Pacific (including Noumea) to Auckland and was linked from New Zealand to Australia by the Trans-Tasman Air Service. Airmail from the New Hebrides could therefore be shipped to either Sydney or to Noumea to join this service. The service was abandoned after the Pearl Harbour attack on 7th December 1941 (Figure 58). The airmail postage from the New Hebrides was calculated by adding the surface rate (Table 8) to the relevant air surcharge (Table 10).

From 1942 to 1946 allied military forces were stationed in the New Hebrides and sent large quantities of airmail to the USA, as well as to New Zealand (see Jersey, S.C., 1994, New Hebrides Military Postal History of the United States Forces, pub. Collectors Club of Chicago). This mail did not, however, pass through the Condominium Post Office.

Figure 58. Air cover to USA. The 1fr 5gc stamps were cancelled by both Vila PM7C and Port-Vila PM11A postmarks (dated 19th December 1941), which paid the 30gc non-colonial letter rate, plus 75gc (up to ½ oz) USA air surcharge (Table 9). [Assuming an exchange rate of 1gf to 2/-, then the 1/7d charge would be 79gc, which was rounded down to 75gc. A surcharge for the Pan American Trans-Pacific air service was not required, as it had ceased after 7th December].

Table 9. Airmail rates from Australia (1938-1945)

Destination	Air letter rate (per ½ ounce)	Air postcard rate
Great Britain (Empire air mail scheme)	1/6d (Until 22/9/38) 5d (23/9/38 to 24/8/39) 1/6d (From 5/9/39)	9d (Until 22/9/38) 3d (23/9/38 to 24/8/39) 9d (From 5/9/39)
Europe (including France)	1/9d (1/8d per additional ½ oz)	11d
U.S.A.	1/7d (1/6d per additional ½ oz)	10d

Table 10. Air surcharges for mail sent via the Trans-Tasman Service and the Pan American Trans-Pacific Service (1940-1941)

Destination	Air surcharge from Sydney (per ¼ ounce)	Air surcharge from Noumea (per 5g)
Australia	-	5fr
New Zealand	?	2fr 25c
New Caledonia	9d	-
Canada	2/9d	10fr 50c
USA	2/9d	10fr 50c
Great Britain (via Canada)	2/9d	?
Great Britain (via USA)	4/-	18fr
France (via USA)	?	19fr

On 1st October 1945 an additional air service was introduced via New Zealand. As a result, airmail could either be flown from the New Hebrides via New Zealand to its destination (Figure 59), or shipped to Sydney and then flown to its destination. The postage was calculated by adding the surface mail charge (Table 8) to the air surcharge (Table 11). As it was quicker at that time to send mail to New Caledonia and the Solomon Islands by ship, no air surcharges are quoted for these destinations in Table 11.

On 16th July 1947 flights began by TRansports Aériens du PAcifique Sud (TRAPAS), which involved a round trip from Noumea to Santo to Port Vila to Noumea. A few months later airmail to Australia (and from there to other destinations westward) could be sent via the TRAPAS service, as it was possible to transfer the mail to a Pan American Service in Noumea, which was then flown to Sydney. It appears that the air surcharges for this service were the same as those subsequently published on 27th September 1947, which are listed in Table 12 (Figure 60). We have seen a letter from the Condominium Postmaster (dated 16th July 1948) in which he quotes the air surcharge to Sweden as 55gc per 5g, which is less than that listed in Table 12. As the latter surcharge was for mail sent via London, it is possible that other air routes to European countries became available after September 1947, which resulted in the charge being reduced.

Table 11. Air surcharges used by the Condominium Post Office (1945-1947)

Destination	1945-1947 (per ½ oz)	
	via New Zealand	via Australia
Australia	25gc	20gc
New Zealand	0	30gc
France	1gf 20gc	95gc
Great Britain	1gf 20gc	95gc
Europe	1gf 20gc	95gc
USA	60gc	35gc

Table 12. Air surcharges used by the Condominium Post Office (1947–1977)

Destination	1947-1953 (per 5g)	1953-1962		1963-1977	
		1st class (per 5g)	2nd class (per 20g)	1st class (per 5g)	2nd class (per 20g)
Pacific area					
Australia	15gc	10gc	20gc	10gc	10gc
New Zealand	25gc	10gc	15gc	10gc	10gc
New Caledonia	5gc	5gc	5gc	5gc	5gc
Fiji	25gc	15gc	20gc	5gc	5gc
Samoa	25gc	15gc	20gc	15gc	15gc
Solomon Islands	-	15gc	20gc	5gc	5gc
Tonga	25gc	15gc	20gc	15gc	15gc
Europe					
France	50gc	45gc	55gc	45gc	45gc
Great Britain	50gc	50gc	60gc	45gc	45gc
Europe	60gc(via London)	45gc	55gc	45gc	45gc
Americas					
USA	60gc	35gc	40gc	30gc	30gc
Canada	60gc	40gc	50gc	30gc	30gc
Argentina	85gc	55gc	65gc	40gc	40gc
Brazil	85gc	55gc	65gc	40gc	40gc
Chile	85gc	55gc	65gc	40gc	40gc
Peru	85gc	45gc	55gc	40gc	40gc
Venezuela	85gc	40gc	50gc	30gc	30gc
Central America	70gc	40gc	50gc	30gc	30gc
Caribbean Islands	70gc	40gc	50gc	30gc	30gc
Africa					
Angola	65gc	60gc	75gc	55gc	55gc
Congo	65gc	60gc	75gc	55gc	55gc
Egypt	45gc	40gc	50gc	50gc	50gc
Ethiopia	50gc	50gc	60gc	50gc	50gc
Gambia	60gc	60gc	75gc	55gc	55gc
Gold Coast (Ghana)	65gc	60gc	75gc	55gc	55gc
Ivory Coast	65gc	60gc	75gc	55gc	55gc

Kenya	50gc	50gc	60gc	50gc	50gc
Libya	50gc	50gc	60gc	50gc	50gc
Madagascar	65gc	55gc	65gc	40gc	40gc
Morocco	55gc	50gc	60gc	50gc	50gc
Mozambique	65gc	50gc	60gc	50gc	50gc
Nigeria	65gc	60gc	75gc	55gc	55gc
Rhodesia	55gc	55gc	65gc	55gc	55gc
Senegal	60gc	60gc	75gc	55gc	55gc
Sierra Leone	60gc	60gc	75gc	55gc	55gc
South Africa	60gc	50c	60c	50gc	50gc
Sudan	50gc	45gc	55gc	50gc	50gc
Togo	65gc	60gc	75gc	55gc	55gc
Tunisia	55gc	50gc	60gc	50gc	50gc
Asia					
Burma	30gc	30gc	35gc	30gc	30gc
Ceylon				30gc	30gc
India (Madras)	30gc	30gc	35gc	30gc	30gc
India (Bombay)	35gc	30gc	35gc	30gc	30gc
Malaya	25gc	25gc	30gc	25gc	25gc
Sarawak	25gc	25gc	30gc	25gc	25gc
Middle East					
Aden	50gc	45gc	55gc	40gc	40gc
Cyprus	45gc	40gc	50gc	40gc	40gc
Iran	40gc	40gc	50gc	40gc	40gc
Iraq	40gc	40gc	50gc	40gc	40gc
Lebanon	45gc	40gc	50gc	40gc	40gc
Malta	50gc	45gc	55gc	45gc	45gc
Syria	45gc	40gc	50gc	40gc	40gc
Turkey	50gc	45gc	55gc	40gc	40gc
Orient					
China	80gc	25gc	30gc	25gc	25gc
Hong Kong	30gc	25gc	30gc	25gc	25gc
Japan	40gc	30gc	35gc	30gc	30gc
Philippines	-	25gc	30gc	25gc	25gc

Figure 59. Air cover to France. The 1gf 30gc stamps were cancelled by a Port-Vila Type PM11A postmark (dated 27th December 1945), which paid the 10gc colonial letter rate, plus 1fr 20gc (up to 5g) France air surcharge for mail sent via New Zealand (Table 11). It has a London OAT transit mark on the front.

The 5g air surcharge was applied to postcards sent by airmail. An air letter (aerogramme) service was also introduced in September 1947, with a rate of 30gc (Figure 61).

The TRAPAS service was expanded to include direct flights to and from Sydney, with the inaugural flight from Sydney (via Noumea) arriving in Port Vila on 7th December 1947. From this time, an all-up service was the norm. It appears that from October 1948 the TRAPAS service operated in parallel with direct Qantas flights between Port Vila and Sydney.

New air surcharge rates were introduced on 1st July 1953 (Table 12), which lasted until 31st December 1962. These included a second-class air service. The first-class airmail surcharges were charged per 5g and the second-class air surcharges were charged per 20g (A second-class air service may have been introduced for mail between the New Hebrides and Great Britain in 1949). The air letter (aerogramme) rate was reduced to 25gc in 1953 (Figure 62).

New Hebrides Postal History

Figure 60. Air cover to Australia. The 40gc stamp was cancelled by a Vila Type PM7D postmark (dated 27th April 1950), which paid the 10gc colonial letter rate, plus 30gc (10g) Australia air surcharge (Table 12).

Figure 61. Air letter to France. The 30gc stamp was cancelled by a Vila Type PM7D postmark (dated 7th February 1951), which paid the 1947-1953 air letter rate.

Figure 62. Air letter to USA. The 25gc stamp was cancelled by a Vila Type PM30A postmark (dated ? March 1962), which paid the 1953-1962 air letter rate.

1961-1970

On 1st January 1961 all surface postal rates were increased. The letter rate became 15gc for colonial destinations (Figure 63) and 25gc for non-colonial destinations (Figure 64). The postcard rates were increased to 10gc and 15gc for colonial and non-colonial destinations respectively. A single registration fee (30gc) was adopted for all destinations (Figure 65). These rates lasted until 30th June 1970 (Table 13).

Table 13. Surface postal rates used by the Condominium Post Office (1961 – 1970)

Postal item		Charge
Colonial letter rate	- up to 20g - up to 50g	15gc 25gc
Non-colonial letter rate	- up to 20g - each additional 20g	25gc 15gc
Postcard rate	- Colonial destination - Non-colonial destination	10gc 15gc
Registration fee	- All destinations	30gc

A new set of air surcharges was introduced on 1st January 1963, which were used until 30th June 1977. Charges for the most popular destinations are listed in Table 12 many of which were reduced. Both first and second class rates were reduced to some destinations (for example, Solomon Islands, USA), but in other cases only the second class rates were reduced (for example, France, New Zealand). These charges remained in force until the introduction of the New Hebrides Franc currency in 1977.

Figure 63. Cover to Port Vila. The 15gc stamps were cancelled by the Forari Type PM32A postmark (dated 2nd November 1962), which paid the colonial letter rate. The cachet commemorates the opening of the Forari post office.

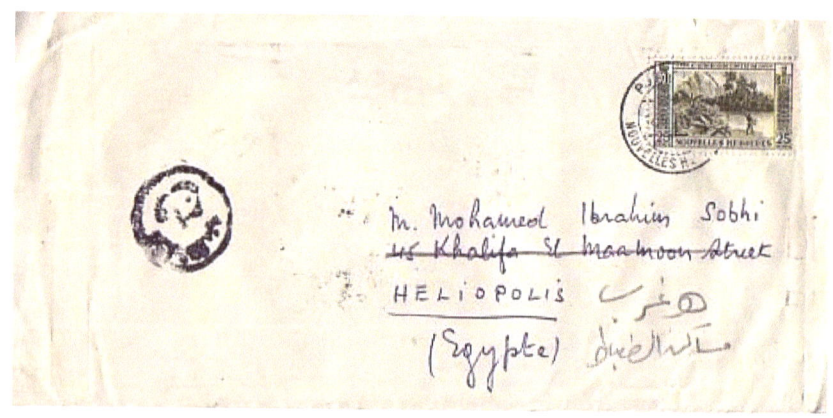

Figure 64. Cover to Egypt. The 25gc stamp was cancelled by the Port-Vila Type PM31A postmark (dated 12thAugust 1963), which paid the non-colonial letter rate.

Figure 65. Registered cover to USA. The 55gc stamps were cancelled by Santo Type PM28A postmark (dated 13th November 1965), which paid the 25gc non-colonial letter rate plus the 30gc registration fee. Registration is indicated by label NR21B.

Postcards (with the correct postage) continue to be uncommon during this period. Although a few were sent by surface mail (Figure 66), most were sent by airmail (Figure 67). In the latter case, the air surcharge was the 5g rate (Table 12).

A dual charge was initially adopted for air letters (aerogrammes) in 1963. The 25gc charge was retained for colonial destinations (Figure 68), but a new 30gc charge was introduced for non-colonial destinations (Figure 69). This dual charge lasted until the change in surface rates in 1970.

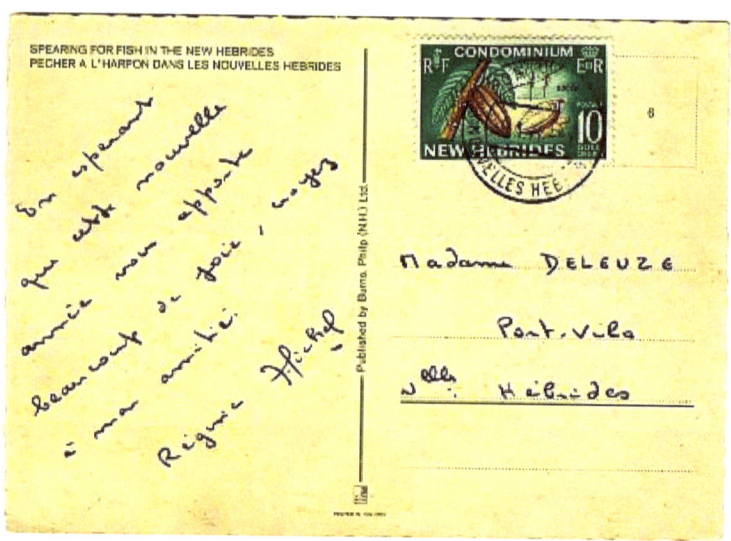

Figure 66. Postcard posted within Port Vila. The 10gc stamp was cancelled by a Port-Vila Type PM31A postmark (dated 9th January 1970), which paid the colonial postcard rate.

Figure 67. Air postcard to France. The 55gc stamps were cancelled by a Santo Type PM28A postmark (dated 24th October 1965), which paid the 10gc colonial postcard rate, plus 45gc (up to 5g) France air surcharge.

New Hebrides Postal History

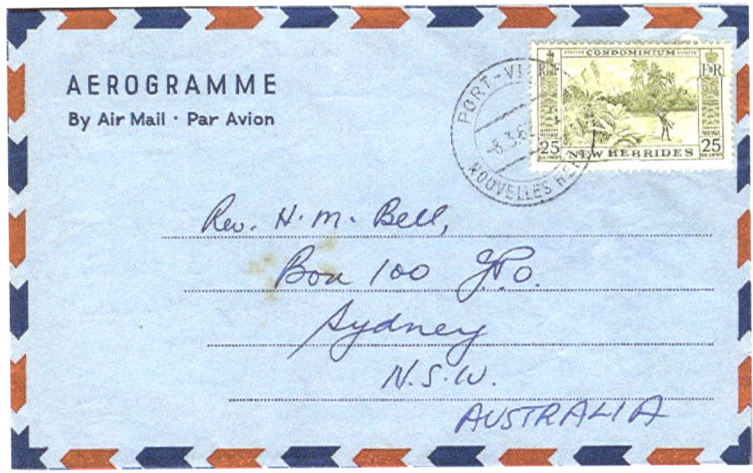

Figure 68. Air letter to Australia. The 25gc stamp was cancelled by a Port-Vila Type PM31A postmark (dated 8th March 1963), which paid the 1963-1970 colonial air letter rate.

Figure 69. Air letter to Germany. The 30gc stamps were cancelled by a Port-Vila postmark Type PM31A postmark (dated 12th January 1963), which paid the 1963-1970 non-colonial air letter rate.

1970-1972

By the 1970s most overseas mail was sent by airmail, with only overweight letters / packets using surface mail. Nevertheless, the surface mail charges were necessary to calculate the correct airmail postage. New surface postal rates were introduced on 1st July 1970, which saw an increase in letter rates to 20gc for colonial (Figure 70) and 30gc for non-colonial (Figure 71) destinations. Postcard rates were increased to 15gc and 25gc for colonial and non-colonial destinations respectively. The registration fee was also increased to 50gc (Figure 72). These rates lasted less than two years until 30th April 1972 (Table 14).

Table 14. Surface postal rates used by the Condominium Post Office (1970 – 1972)

Postal item		Charge
Colonial letter rate	- up to 20g	20gc
	- up to 100g	40gc
Non-colonial letter rate	- up to 20g	30gc
	- each additional 20g	20gc
Postcard rate	- Colonial destination	15gc
	- Non-colonial destination	25gc
Registration	- All destinations	50gc

The air surcharges were those listed in Table 12. However, the dual air letter (aerogramme) rates were unified under a new 35gc rate that lasted until the introduction of the new currency in 1977. A further innovation during this period was the introduction on 13th July 1971 of an aerogramme with a 35gc stamp incorporated into its design (Figure 73).

Figure 70. Cover to Aoba. The 20gc stamp was cancelled by a Santo Type PM47 postmark (dated 15th October 1970), which paid the colonial letter rate.

Figure 71. Cover to USA. The 30gc stamps were cancelled by a Port-Vila Type PM33A postmark (dated 6th July 1970), which paid the non-colonial letter rate.

Figure 72. Registered air cover to Australia. The 80gc stamps were cancelled by a Longana Type PM36B postmark (dated 15th October 1970), which paid the 20gc colonial letter rate, plus 50gc registration fee, plus 10gc (up to 5g) Australia air surcharge. Registration is indicated by label NR25. The cachet commemorates the opening of the Longana post office.

Figure 73. Aerogramme to France. The 35gc aerogramme was cancelled by a Vila Type PM30B postmark (dated 11th January 1973), which paid the 1970-1977 aerogramme rate.

New Hebrides Postal History

1972-1977

On 1st May 1972, new surface rates were introduced (Table 15) and were used until the introduction of the new currency (New Hebrides Franc) on 1st July 1977. The colonial letter and postcard rates increased to 25gc (Figure 74) and 20gc respectively. Although the non-colonial letter rate was increased to 35gc (Figure 75), the postcard rate was unchanged at 25gc. The registration fee was also increased to 60gc (Figure 76).

Figure 74. Cover to Aoba. The 25gc stamps were cancelled by a Port Vila Type PM31B postmark (dated 12th July 1972), which paid the colonial letter rate.

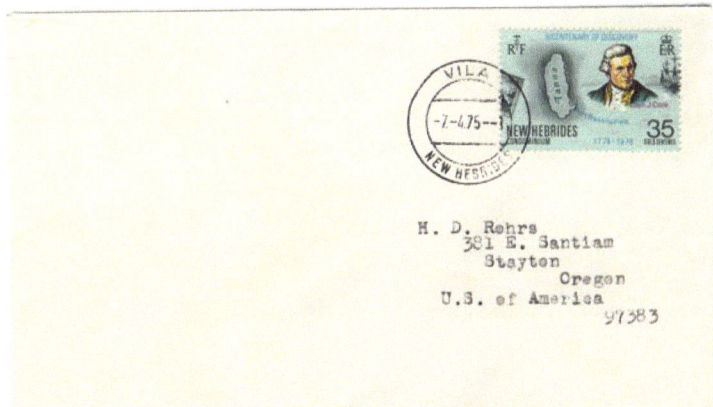

Figure 75. Cover to USA. The 35gc stamp was cancelled by a Port Vila Type PM30B postmark (dated 7th April 1975), which paid the non-colonial letter rate.

The air surcharges were those listed in Table 12 and were used until the introduction of the new currency on 1st July 1977. The aerogramme rate was unaltered at 35gc.

Figure 76. Registered cover to Aoba. The 85gc stamps were cancelled by a Santo Type PM29B postmark (dated 31st January 1975), which paid the 25gc colonial letter rate plus the 60gc registration fee (no air surcharge was needed for a cover flown within the New Hebrides). Registration is indicated by label NR21D.

Table 15. Surface postal rates used by the Condominium Post Office (1972 – 1977)

Postal item		Charge
Colonial letter rate	- up to 20g - up to 50g	25gc 30gc
Non-colonial letter rate	- up to 20g - up to 50g	35gc 65gc
Postcard rate	- Colonial	20gc
	- Non-colonial	25gc
Registration fee	- All destinations	60gc

1977-1980

The introduction of the new currency (New Hebrides Franc – FNH) on 1st July 1977 required that new postal rates be adopted and this resulted in a comprehensive overhaul of the rates (Table 16). These lasted throughout the final years of the New Hebrides Condominium (until 29th July 1980), after which the territory became the Republic of Vanuatu.

A local letter rate was created (Figure 77) and the distinction between colonial and non-colonial destinations abolished. Henceforth, there was only an overseas letter rate. The postcard rate of 10 FNH and the registration fee of 50 FNH applied to both local and overseas mail.

Table 16. Surface postal rates used by the Condominium Post Office (1977 – 1980)

Postal item		Charge
Local letter rate	- up to 20g - up to 50g - up to 100g	10 FNH 20 FNH 30 FNH
Overseas letter rate	- up to 20g - up to 50g - up to 100g	15 FNH 25 FNH 35 FNH
Postcard rate		10 FNH
Registration fee		50 FNH

Although mail was sent by air within the New Hebrides, no air surcharge was payable on this local mail. Air surcharges were applied only to overseas mail, most of which was now sent by airmail. The postage of the latter was calculated by adding the air surcharge (Table 17) to the surface rate (Table 16). The surcharge for airmail was no longer based on individual country destinations. Instead overseas destinations were allocated to one of three regions, depending on their distance from the New Hebrides (Figures 78 - 80). The air surcharge was therefore calculated according to the destination group and weight of item (Table 17). There is evidence that an express airmail service may also have been available for an additional charge. The aerogramme charge was 15 FHN to all destinations. Initially the 1971 aerogramme was overprinted 15FNH (Figure 81), but a new design incorporating a 15FNH stamp was issued on 9th August 1978.

Figure 77. Cover to Port Vila. The 10FNH stamp was cancelled by a Tanna Type PM35C postmark (dated 18th July 1978), which paid the local letter rate.

Table 17. Air surcharges used by the Condominium Post Office (1977 – 1980)

Destination	Letter surcharge (per 10g)	Postcard surcharge
Australasia	5 FNH	5 FNH
North America, South America	15 FNH	10 FNH
Europe (including Great Britain and France), Africa	25 FNH	20 FNH

New Hebrides Postal History

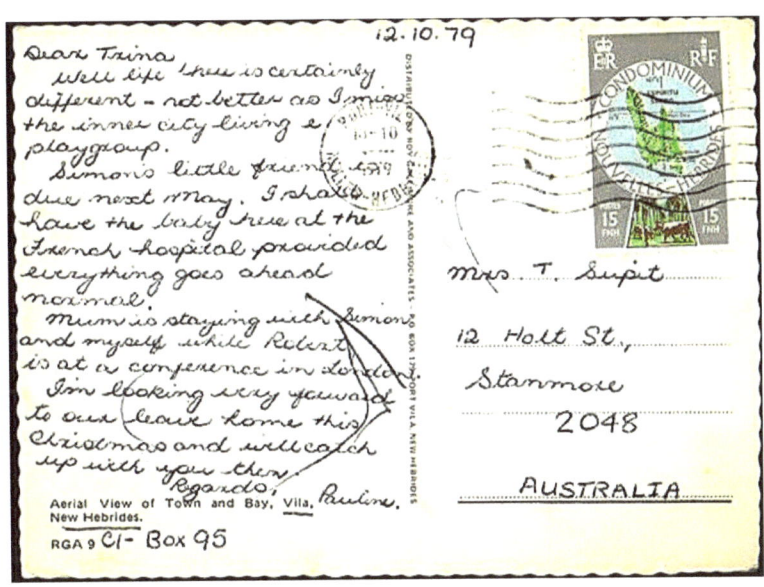

Figure 78. Airmail postcard to Australia. The 15FNH stamp was cancelled by a Port Vila Type PM56 postmark (dated 13th October 1979), which paid the 10FNH postcard rate and the 5FNH postcard air surcharge (Australasia region).

Figure 79. Airmail postcard to the USA. The 20FNH stamp was cancelled by a Port Vila Type PM31B postmark (dated 23rd January 1979), which paid the 10FNH postcard rate and the 10FNH postcard air surcharge (America region).

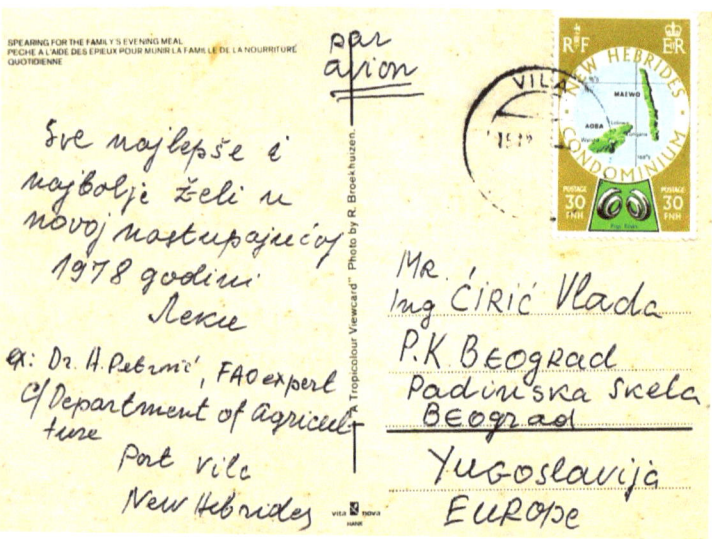

Figure 80. Airmail postcard to Yugoslavia. The 30FNH stamp was cancelled by a Vila Type PM30B postmark (dated 15th December 1977), which paid the 10FNH postcard rate plus the 20FNH postcard air surcharge (Europe / Africa region).

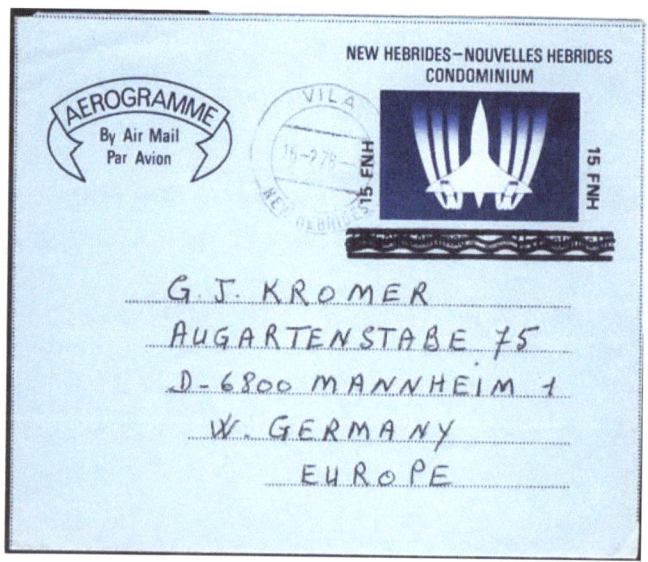

Figure 81. Aerogramme to Germany. The 15FNH provisional aerogramme was cancelled by a Vila Type PM30B postmark (dated 16th February 1978), which paid the 1977-1980 aerogramme rate.

SECTION B

POSTMARKS

A group of men from Ambrym, New Hebrides. Hume postcard series (Number 246), published circa 1905.

New Hebrides Postal History

4. REGULAR POSTMARKS

The postmarks listed in this section are those approved for routine use in the New Hebrides by recognized postal authorities in New South Wales and New Caledonia or by the Condominium Post Office. We designate these marks as PM types.

The purpose of this listing is to show the basic design of postmarks, which for ease of identification, have been arranged chronologically according to their first reported appearance.

Date block variants. The arrangement of the date blocks in postmarks up to the 1940s showed considerable variation. Postmarks are known with the month in italics (Fig. 82A), inverted date (Fig. 82B), parts of the date inverted, such as the well-known inverted '2' of PM2 that occurred throughout 1912 (Fig. 82C) and missing date (Fig. 82D). Many other minor variants in design and evidence of wear exist. This is a complex area, which would interest the specialist.

Figure 82A   *Figure 82B*   *Figure 82C*   *Figure 82D*

Colour variants. Generally, all regular postmarks were applied using black ink (Fig. 82), but there were times when other coloured inks were employed. During 1910 most of the postmarks were applied in blue, but coloured postmarks occurred at various times either in purple (Fig. 83A), blue (Fig. 83B), green (Fig. 83C) or red-brown (Fig. 83D). This is also an area that would benefit from specialist study.

Figure 83A   *Figure 83B*   *Figure 83C*   *Figure 83D*

Shipboard cancellers. Prior to 1950, several postmarks from this island territory were associated with shipboard cancellers. It is therefore useful to summarize what we know of their locations. Although we are confident of the below outline, some aspects need confirmation.

Type **PM1** was transferred to S.S. Malaita when the NSW postal agency was closed and appears to have been used as a shipboard canceller from 1908 until it was retired in 1910. The NC postal agency was operated by Société Française des Nouvelles Hébrides on S.S. Ne Oblie and subsequently S.S. La Perouse from March 1903 to December 1904 and used **PM2** (with **PM3** as a reserve cancel). The postal contract then passed to Messageries Maritime and **PM3** was transferred to S.S. Pacifique and used until 1910. **PM2** may have been retained by S.S. La Perouse and occasionally used (contrary to regulations), until it was transferred to the Condominium Post Office in 1908. Between 1910 and 1924, S.S. Pacifique carried **PM5A** (1910-1915), **PM5B** (1916-1918) and **PM5C** (1919-1924). **PM5C** was briefly used on S.S. Vincent de St. Paul later in 1924, before it was transferred to S.S. Dupleix and used from 1925 to 1928. It was finally transferred to S.S. La Perouse, which carried it from 1928 to 1931, after which it was retired. From 1932 S.S. La Perouse carried **PM8**, which was transferred to S.S. Pierre Loti during the summer of 1936 and then used until October 1938. From 1934 S.S. Bucephale carried **PM10**, but when the ship was lost on a reef on 14th June 1937, this canceller was also transferred to S.S. Pierre Loti. **PM13** was first used on S.S. Pierre Loti in 1937, but only for a few months before being reserved. Instead, **PM8** and **PM10** were used in parallel until October 1938, when they were replaced by **PM14**. Type **PM14** was used until early in 1940 when it was retired and **PM13** again used. This use lasted only a few months because S.S. Pierre Loti was seized by the Free French authorities in August 1940 and taken out of service in the Pacific region. It appears that its cancellers were transferred to the Port Vila Post Office and subsequently used on 'philatelic' covers. Type **PM9A** was carried by S.S. Morinda from 1934 and was replaced by **PM9B** in 1938, which remained in use until probably 1947. A large number of 'philatelic' covers with **PM9B** are known dated 29th November 1949.

Studies of the dates on these postmarks suggest that after ships had collected mail during their interisland journeys, they often cancelled it in one batch on the day the ship arrived in Port Vila.

Type PM1

Type PM1. Vila English postmark consisting of a single circle (diameter 23mm),

This postmark was used by the NSW postal agency from 1892 until 1908 when the agency was closed. It was then transferred to S.S. Malaita and used as a shipboard canceller from 1908 (it is unclear whether it was subsequently transferred to and used by the Port Vila Post Office) until it was retired in 1910. There have been reported variations in the diameter of this cancel and of a short leg of the 'H'. Computer analysis of these varieties leads us to conclude that these are artefacts resulting from variations in the application of the cancel and that there was only a single PM1 canceller. Faked examples are known (see Type PU4).

Type PM2

Type PM2. Port-Vila French postmark consisting of an outer circle (diameter 23mm) and an inner circle (diameter 13mm) of 20 dashes.

Type PM2 was used by the NC postal agency, which was based on S.S. Ne Oblie and then S.S. La Perouse from March 1903 until December 1904. After this date the postal contract was awarded to Messageries Maritimes and its use became sporadic (and possibly contrary to regulations) until being transferred to the Condominium Post Office in 1908. It was then used until 1924 when it was replaced with Type PM6. Faked examples of this postmark are known (see Type PU7).

Type PM3

Type PM3. Port Sandwich French postmark consisting of an outer circle (diameter 21mm) and an inner ring (diameter 12.5mm) of 34 dots.

Type PM3 was initially the reserve canceller of the NC postal agency, which was operated by Société Française des Nouvelles Hébrides on S.S. Ne Oblie and subsequently S.S. La Perouse. When the postal contract passed to Messageries Maritimes in December 1904, PM3 was transferred to S.S. Pacifique. It was then used until 1910 when Type PM5A replaced it. Faked examples of this postmark are known (see Type PU8).

Type PM4

Type PM4. Vila English postmark consisting of a single circle (diameter 25.5mm).

Type PM4 was introduced in 1909 as an English canceller to complement Type PM2. Unlike PM1, it has the town name at the top and territory name at the bottom, which may have been intended to rationalize the design of the two postmarks used by the Condominium Post Office in Port Vila. Type PM6 replaced it in 1924. Faked examples of this postmark are known (see Type PU9).

Type PM5A   *Type PM5B*   *Type PM5C*

Type PM5. Service Maritime French postmarks were carried on interisland vessels. Type PM5A had an outer circle (diameter 24mm) and an inner circle (diameter 14mm) comprising 30 dots. Type PM5B had an outer circle (diameter 23mm) and an inner circle (diameter 14mm) of 35 dots (not 36 dots). Type PM5C is the same cancel as PM5B, but with a new date block. The latter is positioned higher and the year is shown as two numerals, not four as with PM5B.

Type PM5A replaced Type PM3 in 1910 and was used until 1915. It was replaced by PM5B in 1916, which was replaced by Type PM5C in 1919. The cancels were carried on S.S. Pacifique until October 1924. PM5C was transferred to S.S. Vincent de St. Paul (during late 1924), then to S.S. Dupleix (1925 to 1928) and finally to S.S. La Perouse (1928 to 1931).

 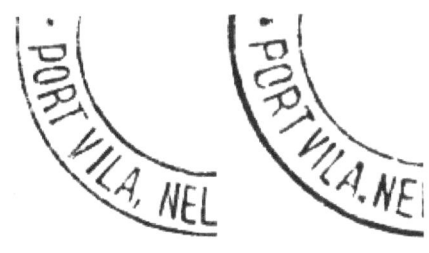

Type PM6.   *Figure 84*

Type PM6. Port Vila French Postes Condominium postmark, consisting of a double circle (diameters 29mm / 19mm).

Type PM6 was introduced in 1924 to replace Types PM2 and PM4 and was the only Port Vila postmark in use until 1928. Its subsequent use was intermittent until it was retired in 1931. A second canceller with smaller lettering (Figure 84, left) was used between June 1924 and April 1925, but the difference with the main canceller (Figure 84, right) is insufficient to justify defining this as a separate design sub-type.

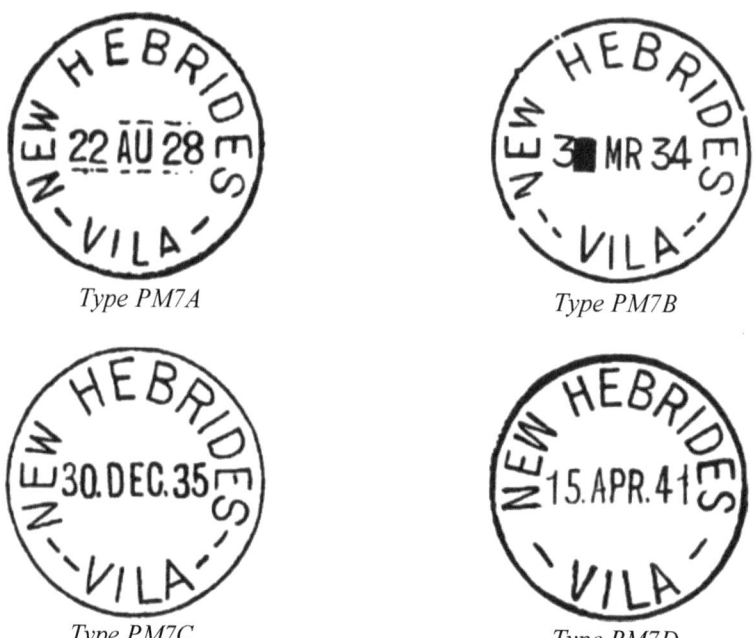

Type PM7A

Type PM7B

Type PM7C

Type PM7D

Type PM7. Vila English postmark consisting of a single circle (diameter 30mm).

Type PM7 was introduced in 1927 and continued in use until 1951. It was the only Port Vila postmark in use between December 1931 and August 1935. During the 24 years life of this design, four cancellers have been identified, which are sufficiently distinctive to be regarded as sub-types. Type PM7A has single line separators between NEW HEBRIDES and VILA and the month represented by two letters. It was used between 1927 and 1932. Type PM7B has double separators and the month represented by two letters. This canceller is also characterized by a short leg of 'N'. It was used between 1931 and 1939. Type PM7C has double separators and the month represented by three letters. It was used between 1935 and 1947. Type PM7D has single separators and the month represented by three letters. It was used between 1940 and 1951.

Variants of PM7B and PM7C have been reported with single separators (of varying length) instead of double separators. Computer analysis demonstrates that these are artefacts, probably resulting from over-inking. Variations in the length of the single separators of PM7A and PM7D have been reported, but these are artefacts (also see Table 27 footnote).

Type PM8

Type PM8. Interisland Service English postmark consisting of a single circle (diameter 30mm).

This cancel was initially carried on S.S. La Perouse and was in use between 1932 and 1936. In 1936 it was transferred to S.S. Pierre Loti and was used until 1938. Any covers with this cancel after 1938 are probably 'philatelic'. Faked examples of this postmark are known (see PU10).

Type PM9A   *Type PM9B*

Type PM9. Inter-Island English postmark. PM9A consists of a single circle (diameter 30mm) and has no dividers. Type PM9B consists of a single circle (diameter 29mm) and has diamond dividers between NEW HEBRIDES and INTER-ISLAND.

Type PM9A was carried on S.S. Morinda from 1934 and was replaced by PM9B in 1938, which remained in use probably until 1947 (Though a considerable amount of 'philatelic' mail was produced with this postmark dated 29th November 1949). A faked example of PM9A is known (see PU11).

Type PM10

Type PM10. Inter-Isles English postmark, consisting of a single circle (diameter 30mm).

This was carried on S.S. Bucephale from 1934, but when the ship was lost on a reef on 14th June 1937, the canceller was transferred to S.S. Pierre Loti (or possibly S.S. Polynesien). It was subsequently used until October 1938, when PM14 replaced it.

Type PM11A   *Type PM11B*

Type PM11. Port Vila French postmark consisting of a double circle (diameters 29mm / 20mm).

Type PM11A has an inner circle of 42 dashes and the date in French. It was in use from 1935 to 1948.

Type PM11B has a solid inner circle and the date in English. It was in use from 1939 to 1951. It is not known why there was an overlap in the use of these two subtypes.

New Hebrides Postal History

PM12A

PM12B

Type PM12. New Hebrides paquebot postmark, consisting of a single circle (diameter 30mm). This is a single canceller, but with interchangeable date slugs. Type PM12A used an English date and Type PM12B a French date.

These subtypes were apparently used in parallel and were the first New Hebrides paquebot marks. They were located in Port Vila and used from 1936 until 1951, when they were replaced by PM17. Other paquebot marks are known from the 1930s to 1950s, but these were unauthorized (see Types PU12 - PU15).

Type PM13

Type PM13. SCE Interinsulaire French postmark consisting of a double circle (diameters 25mm / 13mm) with the inner circle of 19 dashes.

This cancel was carried on S.S. Pierre Loti and used briefly in 1937 before being reserved. It replaced PM14 early in 1940 and was used for a few months before the Free French authorities seized the ship late in the summer of 1940. It was transferred to the Condominium Post Office in August 1940 and its use on covers from that date is 'philatelic'.

Type PM14

Type PM14. Inter-Isles French postmark, consisting of a single circle (diameter 30mm).

This replaced PM8 and PM10 on S.S. Pierre Loti after October 1938 and was used until the early months of 1940 when it was replaced by PM13. It was transferred to the Condominium Post Office in August 1940 and its use on covers from that date is 'philatelic'.

Type PM15   *Type PM16*

A new post office was opened in Luganville, Espiritu Santo on 1st January 1940, which was called Santo.

Type PM15. Santo English postmark, consisting of a single circle (diameter 30mm). It was used from 1940 to 1952.

Type PM16. Santo French postmark, consisting of a double circle (diameters 29mm / 19mm). The inner circle is a series of small dots. Postmarks in which the inner circle appears to be a solid line are due to over-inking. Examples are known with the date 1934 or 1939, but these are errors in date slug settings. It was used from 1940 to 1955.

Type PM17

Type PM17. New Hebrides paquebot cancel consisting of a single circle (diameter 30mm). This replaced PM12 in 1951 and was used until 1975 when it was replaced by PM48. Sporadic later use up to 1977 is known. It was based in Port Vila.

Type PM18A   *Type PM18B*

Type PM18. Vila English postmark, consisting of a single circle (diameter 30mm).

Type PM18A was introduced in 1952 and used until 1959.

Type PM18B contained a time in the date slug and was used for airmail from 1952 until probably 1953.

Type PM19A   *Type PM19B*

Type PM19. Port Vila French postmark, consisting of a double circle.

Type PM19A was a double circle (diameters 30mm / 20mm), which was introduced in 1952 and used until 1959. Two cancellers may have existed because it has occasionally been reported with a dot between the month and year.

Type PM19B was a double circle (diameters 31mm / 22mm), which contained a time in the date slug and was used for airmail from 1952 to 1959.

Type PM20   *Type PM21*

Type PM20. Santo English postmark, consisting of a single circle (diameter 30mm). It was in use between 1952 and 1959.

Type PM21. Santo French postmark, consisting of a double circle (diameters 30mm / 20mm). It was in use from 1952 to 1959.

In 1957 a set of roller cancels were introduced that consisted of a series of double circle date stamps (diameters 29mm / 20mm) separated by six wavy lines. These cancels were intended for use on parcels and business mail containing printed papers. They were used until 1978.

Type PM22

Type PM22. Vila English roller cancel. It was used from 1957 until 1978 when it was replaced by PM51.

Type PM23

Type PM23. Port-Vila French roller cancel. It was used from 1957 until 1978 when it was replaced by PM52.

Type PM24

Type PM24. Santo English roller cancel. It was used from 1957 until 1978 when it was replaced by PM53.

Type PM25

Type PM25. Santo French roller cancel. It was used from 1957 until 1978 when it was replaced by PM54.

From the late 1950s the design of most of the postmarks required for regular use in the New Hebrides was standardized. The double circle design that had been used for the 1957 roller cancels was adopted. Three subtypes were used until Independence in 1980. These can be distinguished as follows:
Subtype A – Double circle (diameters 28mm/20mm) with larger letters. This subtype was introduced at various times from 1958, depending on the post office. It was replaced by subtype B.
Subtype B – Double circle (diameters 28mm/20mm) with smaller letters. This subtype was introduced on 15th October 1970 and used until 1978.
Subtype C – Double circle (diameters 29mm/19mm) with larger letters and a new date block design. This replaced subtype B around May 1978 and was used until Independence in 1980.

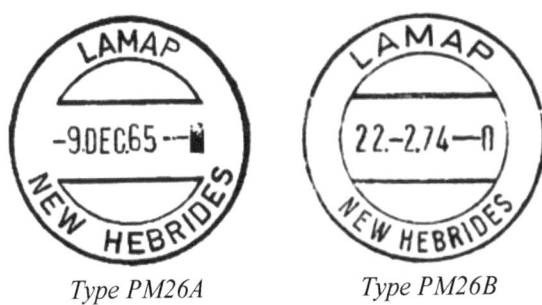

Type PM26A   *Type PM26B*

Type PM26. Lamap English postmark. The Lamap postal agency was opened on 8th October 1958 and operated (with a brief interruption between mid-1960 to mid-1962) until 29th March 1978. It therefore had no subtype C postmark. Type PM26A has an incomplete inner circle, which may have been a design error.

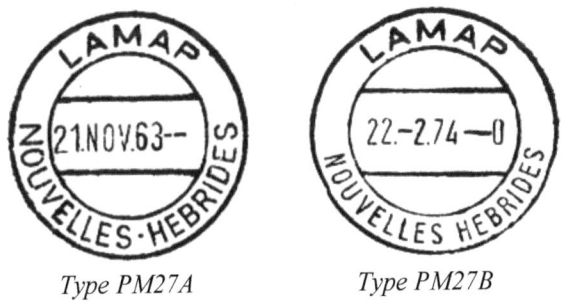

Type PM27A   *Type PM27B*

Type PM27. Lamap French postmark.

Type PM28A   *Type PM28B*   *Type PM28C*

Type PM28. Santo English postmark. The double circle date stamp design was first introduced in 1959.

Type PM29A   *Type PM29B*   *Type PM29C*

Type PM29. Santo French postmark.

Type PM30A   *Type PM30B*   *Type PM30C*

Type PM30. Vila English postmark. The double circle date stamp was first introduced in 1959.

New Hebrides Postal History

| Type PM31A | Type PM31B | Type PM31C |

Type PM31. Port-Vila French postmark.

Type PM32A

Type PM32. Forari English postmark. A new post office opened at Forari, Efate on 2nd November 1962 and operated until early 1969. It therefore had only a subtype A postmark.

Type PM33A

Type PM33. Forari French postmark. Two variants are known, one with the month indicated by three letters and, from July 1964, with the month indicated by numerals.

Type PM34A *Type PM34B* *Type PM34C*

Type PM34. Tanna English postmark. A new post office opened at Isangel, Tanna on 15th February 1963, which was called Tanna.

Type PM35A *Type PM35B* *Type PM35C*

Type PM35. Tanna French postmark.

Type PM36B

Type PM36. Longana English postmark. A new post office opened at Longana, Aoba on 15th October 1970. The post office was called Longana but changed its name to Lolowai on 29th March 1978. It therefore only has a subtype B postmark.

Type PM37B

Type PM37. Longana French postmark.

Type PM38B

Type PM38. Melsisi English postmark. A new post office was opened at Melsisi, Pentecost on 23rd November 1972 and closed on 29th March 1978. It therefore has only a subtype B postmark.

Type PM39B

Type PM39. Melsisi French postmark.

Type PM40B   *Type PM40C*

Type PM40. Norsup English postmark. A new post office was opened at Norsup, Malekula on 15th September 1975. Type PM40B was replaced by PM40C in May 1978

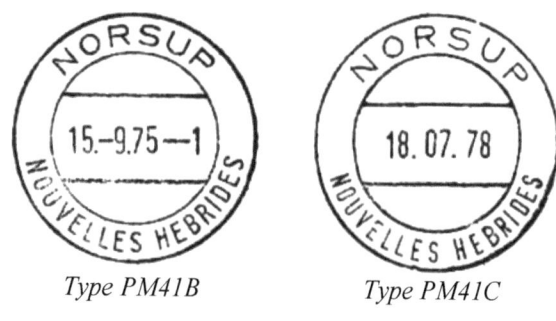

Type PM41B   *Type PM41C*

Type PM41. Norsup French postmark.

Type PM42C

Type PM42. Lolowai English postmark. The Longana post office changed its name to Lolowai and issued a new postmark on 30th March 1978. It therefore has only a subtype C postmark.

Type PM43C

Type PM43. Lolowai French postmark.

Type PM44C

Type PM44. Tongoa English postmark. A new post office opened at Morua, Tongoa on 10th May 1976, which was called Tongoa. Initially a single circle provisional postmark was issued (see Type PM49), but this was replaced on 3rd March 1978 by the double circle subtype C postmark.

Type PM45C

Type PM45. Tongoa French postmark, which replaced Type PM50.

Type PM46   *Type PM47*

Type PM46. Santo English provisional postmark consisting of a single circle (diameter 31mm). This was introduced on 29th April 1969 and used until 14th October 1970. The reason for introducing this cancel is unclear. It appears to have been subsequently relocated to the Philatelic Bureau in Port Vila and used on commemorative covers until 1978.

Type PM47. Santo French provisional postmark. Its use was the same as PM46.

PAQUEBOT

Type PM48

Type PM48. Port Vila paquebot mark consisting of an unboxed straight PAQUEBOT measuring 33mm by 4mm. This mark cancelled the stamps and was used in combination with an appropriate Port Vila postmark. It replaced Type PM17 in 1975 and was used until Independence in 1980. A similar, but fake, paquebot mark has been reported on ship mail landed at Santo (see PU15).

New Hebrides Postal History

Type PM49   *Type PM50*

Type PM49. Tongoa English provisional postmark consisting of a single circle (diameter 31mm). This was introduced on 10th May 1976 when the new post office opened. The postmark was replaced by Type PM44C on 3rd March 1978.

Type PM50. Tongoa French provisional postmark. This was introduced when the post office opened in 1976 and was replaced by Type PM45C in 1978.

The design for the roller cancels was changed in May 1978. The new format consisted of a continuous strip of single circle date stamps (diameter 28mm) separated by six wavy lines.

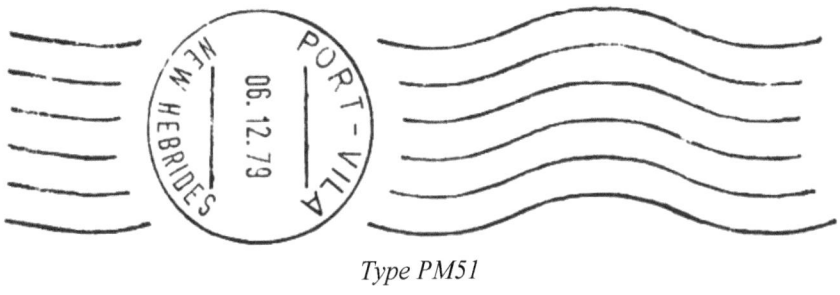

Type PM51

Type PM51. Port-Vila English roller cancel. This was introduced in May 1978 to replace Type PM22 and was used until Independence in 1980. It was the first English postmark to use the name Port Vila.

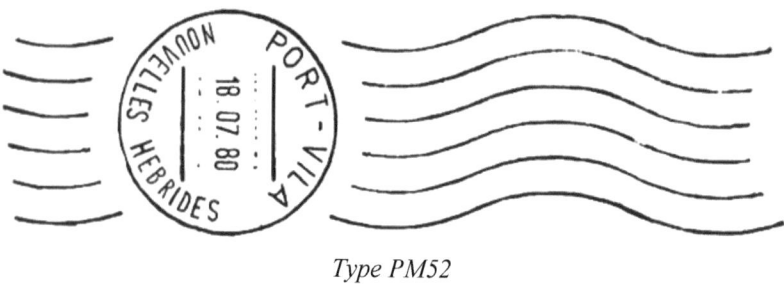

Type PM52

Type PM52. Port-Vila French roller cancel, which was the French equivalent of PM51. It was introduced in May 1978 to replace Type PM23 and was used until Independence in 1980.

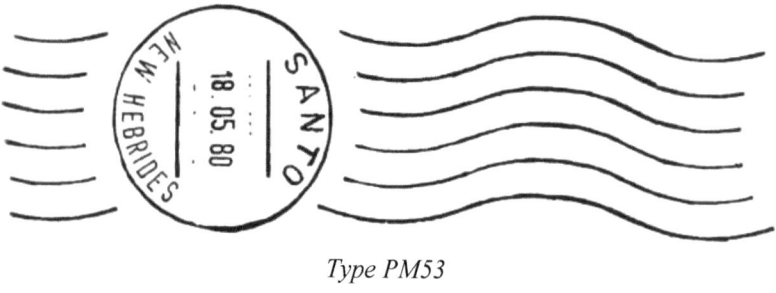

Type PM53

Type PM53. Santo English roller cancel. It was introduced in 1978 to replace Type PM24 and was used until Independence in 1980.

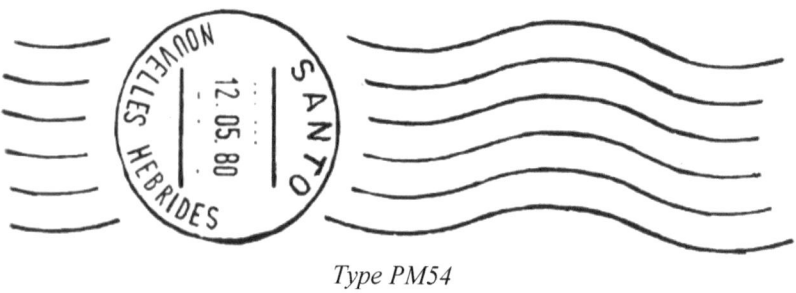

Type PM54

Type PM54. Santo French roller cancel. It was introduced in 1978 to replace Type PM25 and was used until Independence in 1980.

On the 2nd May 1979 the Condominium Post Office introduced a Pitney Bowes machine type 3920, which was used for machine cancelling of mail. Initially this was used for Types PM55 and PM56, which consisted of a single circle date stamp (diameter 22mm) and an adjacent group of seven wavy lines. Variations of this design occurred during the following year. These included the wavy lines being replaced by slogans (Types PS41 – PS46), or the circular date stamp replaced by postage-paid marks (Types PP7 – PP10), or by both (Type PP11).

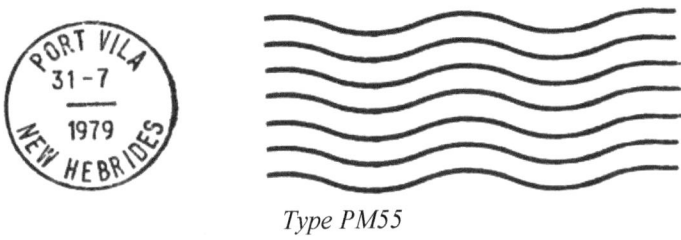

Type PM55

Type PM55. Port Vila English machine cancel. It was introduced on 7th May 1979 and used until Independence.

Type PM56

Type PM56. Port Vila French machine cancel. It was introduced on 8th May 1979 and used until Independence in 1980. A similar unauthorized version is known with five wavy lines (see Type PU16).

Scarcity of postmarks. The relative scarcity of postmarks is a difficult issue to address. Our approach to this problem has been to first divide the New Hebrides postmarks into pre-1941 and 1941-1980 groups. Any postmarks whose use straddled these two periods are considered as part of the 1941-1980 group.

We have examined the relative frequency of pre-1941 postmarks in a sample of approximately 800 covers and postcards. If the 15 postmark subtypes that were used (exclusively) during this period were equally prevalent, then one might expect over 50 examples of each postmark to occur in our sample. We therefore class any postmark that occurs 50 or more times to be 'common'. Any postmark that occurs 25-49 times as 'uncommon', or 5-24 times as 'scarce', or less than 5 times as 'rare' (Table 18). The frequent assertion that Port Sandwich Type PM3 is the rarest New Hebrides postmark is not true. This is evidenced not only by our study, but also by how often it occurs in dealers' stocks. By contrast, the SCE Interinsulaire Type PM13 postmark is genuinely difficult to find.

The influx of large numbers of American military forces in World War II generated a considerable amount of mail and the subsequent years saw increasing numbers of 'philatelic' covers. Most of the post-1940 postmarks are readily available on such mail, though the purist may find it difficult to obtain commercial covers with some of these 'common' postmarks (for example, PM49 and PM50). We have also estimated the relative scarcity of the few post-1940 postmarks that are not 'common' and include them in Table 18.

Table 18. Scarcity of New Hebrides PM type postmarks

Scarcity	PM Types
Rare	PM13
Scarce	PM5B, PM8, PM9A, PM10, PM14, PM18B, PM19B
Uncommon	PM1, PM3, PM5A, PM5C, PM12, PM17, PM26A
Common	All other postmarks

5. SPECIAL POSTMARKS

The postmarks listed in this section were authorized by the Condominium Post Office and used for short periods for special events. They were either first day of issue / premier jour d'emission postmarks or slogan postmarks. We designate these postmarks as PS types.

Type PS1

Type PS1. Vila English first day of issue postmark.

Type PS2

Type PS2. Port Vila French equivalent of PS1.

Types PS1 and PS2 consisted of a single circle date stamp (diameter 24mm) and an adjacent FIRST DAY OF ISSUE or PREMIER JOUR D'EMISSION slogan. They were used for the following postage stamp issues:

20/10/1956	50th anniversary of Condominium
3/9/1957	Definitives
2/9/1963	Freedom from hunger
2/9/1963	Red Cross centenary
25/11/1963	Definitives (15gc, 30gc, 50gc, 2gf)
17/5/1965	International telecommunication union centenary
16/8/1965	Definitives (10gc, 20gc, 40gc, 3gf)
24/10/1965	International cooperation year
24/1/1966	Churchill commemoration

From 1966 until Independence a standardized design was adopted for Port Vila English First Day of Issue and French Premier Jour D'Emission postmarks, which were used for most new issues of postage stamps (For single issue illustrated postmarks see Types PS9 – PS40). There are four subtypes.

Type PS3A

Type PS3B

Type PS3C

Type PS3D

Type PS3. Vila English first day of issue postmark.

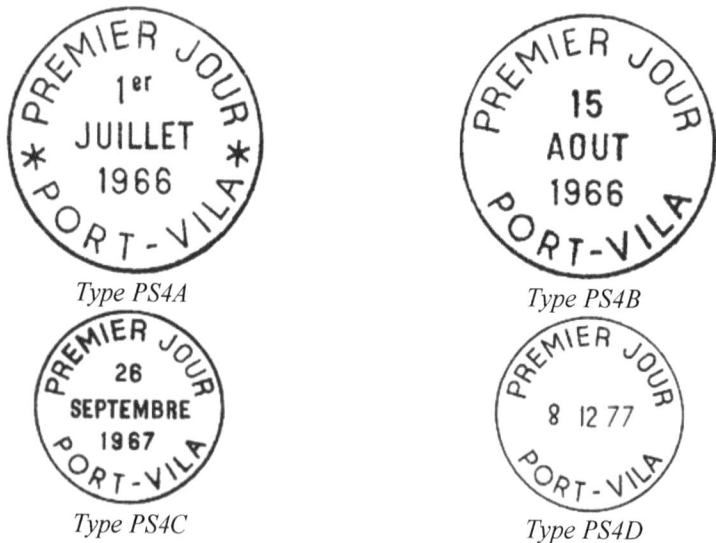

Type PS4A

Type PS4B

Type PS4C

Type PS4D

Type PS4. Port-Vila French equivalents of Type PS3.

Subtype A- Single circle (diameter 30mm) with star separators between FIRST DAY OF ISSUE / PREMIER JOUR and VILA / PORT-VILA. It was used on the following stamp issue:

1/7/1966   Football World Cup finals

Subtype B- Single circle (diameter 30mm) with no separators. It was used on the following stamp issues:

15/8/1966   Definitives (5gc, 25gc, 1gf)
20/9/1966   World Health Organisation
1/12/1966   UNESCO
24/1/1967   Definitive (5gf)
5/12/1967   Definitive (60gc)

Subtype C- Single circle (diameter 22mm) with no separators. It was used on the following stamp issues:

26/9/1967   World War II
(Type PS3B has also been reported used on this issue).
23/5/1968   Bicentenary of Bougainville's voyage
5/8/1968   Definitives (10gc, 20gc, 3gf)
(Only PS4C was used with these redesigned French stamps)
9/10/1968   Concorde
30/6/1969   Timber industry
13/8/1969   South Pacific Games
15/10/1969   Land divers of Pentecost
20/5/1970   New UPU headquarters
30/11/1970   Christmas
13/7/1971   South Pacific Games
13/7/1971   Aerogramme (15gc)
7/9/1971   Royal Society expedition to New Hebrides
23/11/1971   Christmas
24/7/1972   Definitives
25/9/1972   Christmas
26/2/1973   New Hebrides orchids

14/5/1973	New Vila wharf
13/8/1973	Tanna Island
11/2/1974	New Hebrides wildlife
5/8/1975	World scout jamboree
11/11/1975	Christmas
30/1/1976	Concorde
31/3/1976	Centenary of the invention of the telephone
29/6/1976	Constitutional changes
8/11/1976	Christmas
7/2/1977	Silver Jubilee of Queen Elizabeth
1/7/1977	Provisional definitives
7/9/1977	Definitives

Subtype D- Single circle (diameter 22mm) with no separators, but new date block. The English postmark has Port-Vila instead of Vila. It was used on the following stamp issues:

23/11/1977	Definitives
8/12/1977	Christmas
9/5/1978	Definitives
9/5/1978	Concorde
9/8/1978	Aerogramme (15FNH)
1/12/1978	Christmas
11/1/1979	Self-government
10/9/1979	Rowland Hill centenary
4/12/1979	Festival of arts
4/12/1979	Christmas
27/2/1980	New Hebrides birds

New Hebrides Postal History

From 1966 until 1974 a standardized design was adopted for Santo English First Day of Issue and French Premier Jour D'Emission postmarks, which were used for many new issues of postage stamps (For single issue illustrated postmarks see Types PS7 – PS28). Santo special postmarks are represented by only subtypes A and C, as subtypes B and D were not adopted.

Type PS5A   Type PS5C

Type PS5. Santo English first day of issue postmark.

Type PS6A   Type PS6C

Type PS6. Santo French premier jour postmark.

Subtype A- Single circle (diameter 30mm) with star separators between FIRST DAY OF ISSUE / PREMIER JOUR and SANTO. It was used on the following stamp issue:

1/12/1966	UNESCO
26/9/1967	World War II
5/12/1967	Definitive (60gc)
23/5/1968	Bicentenary of Bougainville's voyage
5/8/1968	Definitives (10gc, 20gc, 3gf)

(Only PS6A was used with these redesigned French stamps)

9/10/1968	Concorde

Subtype C- Single circle (diameter 22mm) with no separators. It was used on the following stamp issues:

30/6/1969	Timber industry
13/8/1969	South Pacific Games
15/10/1969	Land divers of Pentecost
20/5/1970	New UPU headquarters
30/11/1970	Christmas
13/7/1971	South Pacific Games
13/7/1971	Aerogramme (35gc)
7/9/1971	Royal Society expedition to New Hebrides
23/11/1971	Christmas
24/7/1972	Definitives
25/9/1972	Christmas
26/2/1973	New Hebrides orchids
14/5/1973	New Vila wharf
13/8/1973	Tanna Island

From 1972 to 1978 a series of illustrated postmarks (diameter 36mm) were adopted for certain stamp issues, instead of the standardized First Day of Issue / Premier Jour postmarks. Up to 1974 these postmarks are known from both Santo and Vila, but thereafter are only known from Vila. It is unclear why illustrated postmarks were used for some stamp issues and not for others.

Type PS7   Type PS8

Type PS7. Santo English First Day of Issue illustrated postmark for the Free French commemorative stamp issue (dated 20th July 1970).

Type PS8. Santo French equivalent of PS7.

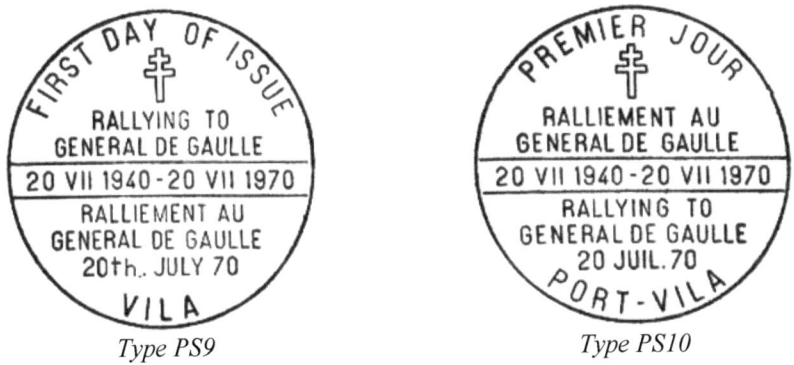

Type PS9   Type PS10

Type PS9. Vila English First Day of Issue illustrated postmark for the Free French commemorative stamp issue (dated 20th July 1970).

Type PS10. Port Vila French equivalent of PS9.

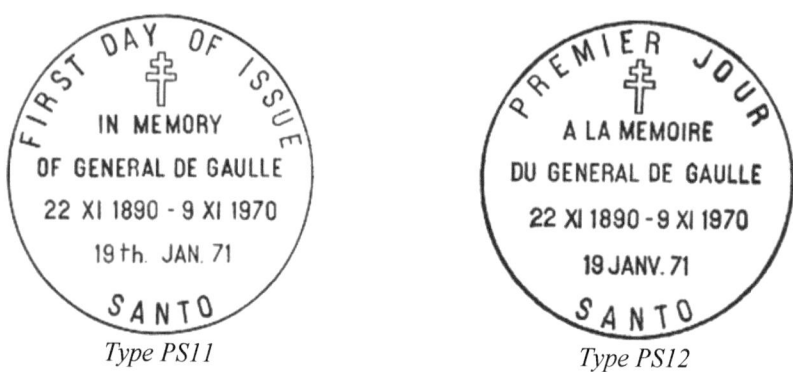

Type PS11   *Type PS12*

Type PS11. Santo English First Day of Issue illustrated postmark for the Death of General De Gaulle stamp issue (dated 19th January 1971).

Type PS12. Santo French equivalent of PS11.

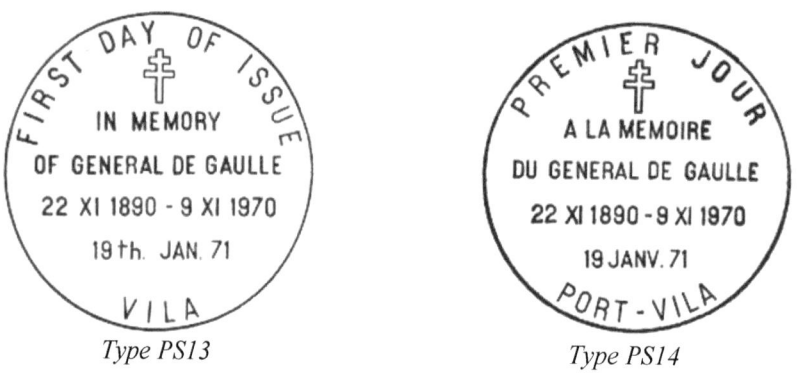

Type PS13   *Type PS14*

Type PS13. Vila English First Day of Issue illustrated postmark for the Death of General De Gaulle stamp issue (dated 19th January 1971).

Type PS14. Port Vila French equivalent of PS13.

New Hebrides Postal History

Type PS15

Type PS16

Type PS15. Santo English First Day of Issue illustrated postmark for the Aircraft commemorative stamp issue (dated 29th February 1972).

Type PS16. Santo French equivalent of PS15.

Type PS17

Type PS18

Type PS17. Vila English First Day of Issue illustrated postmark for the Aircraft commemorative stamp issue (dated 29th February 1972).

Type PS18. Port Vila French equivalent of PS17.

Type PS19   *Type PS20*

Type PS19. Santo English First Day of Issue illustrated postmark for the Royal Silver Wedding stamp issue (dated 20th November 1972).

Type PS20. Santo French equivalent of PS19.

Type PS21   *Type PS22*

Type PS21. Vila English First Day of Issue illustrated postmark for the Royal Silver Wedding stamp issue (dated 20th November 1972).

Type PS22. Port Vila French equivalent of PS21.

Type PS23   *Type PS24*

Type PS23. Santo English First Day of Issue illustrated postmark for the Christmas stamp issue (dated 19th November 1973).

Type PS24. Santo French equivalent of PS23.

Type PS25   *Type PS26*

Type PS25. Vila English First Day of Issue illustrated postmark for the Christmas stamp issue (dated 19th November 1973).

Type PS26. Port Vila French equivalent of PS25.

Type PS27   Type PS28

Type PS27. Santo English First Day of Issue illustrated postmark for the Visit of Queen Elizabeth stamp issue (dated 11th February 1974).

Type PS28. Santo French equivalent of PS27.

Type PS29   Type PS30

Type PS29. Vila English First Day of Issue illustrated postmark for the Visit of Queen Elizabeth stamp issue (dated 11th February 1974).

Type PS30. Port Vila French equivalent of PS29.

These cancels are also known used in error on the New Hebrides Wildlife issue, which was released on the same day.

New Hebrides Postal History

Type PS31 *Type PS32*

Type PS31. Vila English First Day of Issue illustrated postmark for the New Vila Post Office stamp issue (dated 6th May 1974).

Type PS32. Port Vila French equivalent of PS31.

Type PS33 *Type PS34*

Type PS33. Vila English First Day of Issue illustrated postmark for the Bicentennial of the Discovery of the New Hebrides stamp issue. It was used in conjunction with PM30B (dated 1st August 1974).

Type PS34. Port Vila French equivalent of PS33. It was used in conjunction with PM31B (dated 1st August 1974).

Type PS35   *Type PS36*

Type PS35. Vila English First Day of Issue illustrated postmark for the Centenary of the UPU stamp issue (dated 9th October 1974).

Type PS36. Port Vila French equivalent of PS35.

Type PS37   *Type PS38*

Type PS37. Vila English First Day of Issue illustrated postmark for the Definitive (10gf) stamp issue (dated 19th April 1975).

Type PS38. Port Vila French equivalent of PS37.

New Hebrides Postal History

Type PS39   *Type PS40*

Type PS39. Vila English First Day of Issue illustrated postmark for the 25th Anniversary of the Coronation of Queen Elizabeth stamp issue (dated 2nd June 1978).

Type PS40. Port Vila French equivalent of PS39.

The Pitney Bowes machine (see Page 103) was used to produce slogan cancels that were also designed for short-term use. There were three slogan cancels, which were used with both English and French circular date stamps, before Independence in 1980.

   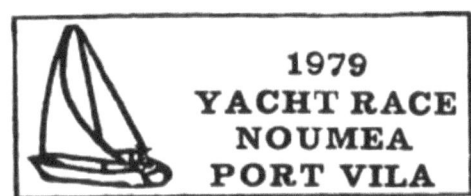

Type PS41

Type PS41. Port Vila English slogan postmark commemorating the Yacht Race between the New Hebrides and New Caledonia. The English and French postmarks were introduced on 3rd July 1979 and then alternated daily until 13th July 1979.

Type PS42

Type PS42. Port Vila French slogan postmark equivalent of PS41.

 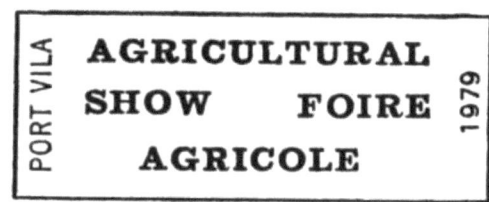

Type PS43.

Type PS43. Port Vila English slogan postmark commemorating the Port Vila Agricultural Show. The English and French postmarks were introduced on 20th August 1979 and then used on alternative days until 29th August 1979.

 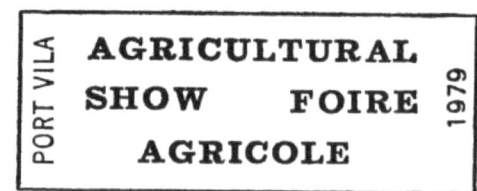

Type PS44

Type PS44. Port Vila French slogan postmark equivalent of Type PS43.

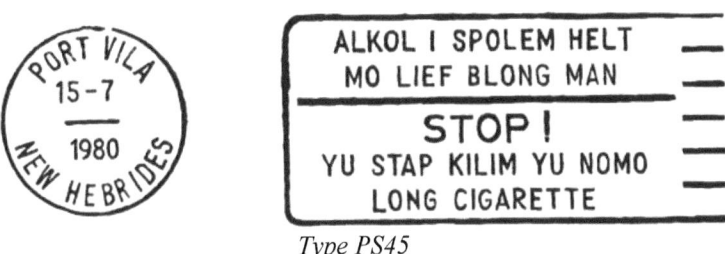

Type PS45

Type PS45. Port Vila English slogan postmark commemorating the Anti-smoking Campaign. The English and French postmarks were introduced on 15th July 1980 and then used on alternative days until Independence.

Type PS46

Type PS46. Port Vila French slogan postmark equivalent of PS45.

Scarcity. Most of the special postmarks are in the common category (see page 104) due to their use on 'philatelic' covers. The Santo illustrated postmarks (PS7-8, PS11-12, PS15-16, PS19-20, PS23-24, PS27-28) and the slogan postmarks, PS45 and PS46, are less easy to find and might fall into the uncommon category.

6. POSTAGE-PAID MARKS

The postmarks listed in this section were authorized by the Condominium Post Office and were used to indicate that postage had been pre-paid and therefore stamps were not required. These include the postage-paid marks used by the Condominium Post Office and other Condominium administrative offices and also the metre marks that were used by various organisations. We designate these marks as PP types.

Type PP1

Type PP1. New Hebrides French POSTE PAYEE mark. Square (26mm high / 25mm wide) hand stamp, known used in 1950 and 1951. This early postage-paid mark was used in association with either a Port Vila or Santo circular date stamp. Its origins are unclear and no English version has been reported.

The 10gc value paid the colonial letter rate. It is unknown whether a 20gc version exists, which would have paid the non-colonial letter rate.

Type PP2A *Type PP2B* *Type PP2C*

Type PP2. Vila English postage-paid marks. These marks were used on official mail from the Condominium Post Office in Port Vila. There are no French equivalent marks.

Type PP2A- Single circle (diameter 27mm) in red or purple, with small lettering in the date block. It was introduced in September 1967 and was replaced by PP2B in 1972.
Type PP2B- Single circle (diameter 27mm) in red, with large lettering in the date block. It was introduced in October 1972 and replaced by PP2C in 1976.
Type PP2C- Single circle (diameter 30mm) in red. It was introduced early in 1976 and was replaced by Types PP3 and PP4 in 1979.

Type PP3 *Type PP4*

Type PP3. Port Vila English postage-paid mark. Double circle (diameters 38mm / 35mm) in red. Introduced early in 1979 to replace PP2C and used until Independence.

Type PP4. Port Vila French postage-paid mark equivalent of PP3.

Meter mail marks were introduced in the mid-1970s and used until Independence in 1980. They consisted of a single circle date stamp (diameter 24.5mm) and a postage-paid square (24mm high x 20mm wide). They were printed in red (Type PP6, SP-100 is also known in black) and mainly used by commercial organizations. The SJ (English cancel) / SP (French cancel) numbers indicated the organization to which the cancel had been allocated.

SP-100: British Administration (only the French PP6 version is known). We have never seen a meter mark used on mail from the French Administration.
SJ-200 / SP-200: Banque de l'Indochine
SJ-201 / SP-201: Burns Philip Co Ltd
SJ-202 / SP-202: Australia New Zealand Bank

Type PP5

Type PP5. Port Vila English meter mail mark.

Type PP6

Type PP6. Port Vila French meter mail mark. Unlike PP5, it also had the time printed between the circular date stamp and the postage-paid square.

The Pitney Bowes machine (see Page 103) was used to produce postage paid marks from May 1979 until Independence the following year (Types PP7 – PP11). We have been unable to clarify the circumstances under which the different cancels (PP3 – PP4 and PP7 – PP11) were used.

It was possible for the postage-paid marks to include a slogan (as used with PS41 – PS46) rather than the wavy lines. Although four postage-paid circular date stamps and three slogans could theoretically produce 12 different types, we have only seen one (Type PP11). This may have been a trial, which was not extended.

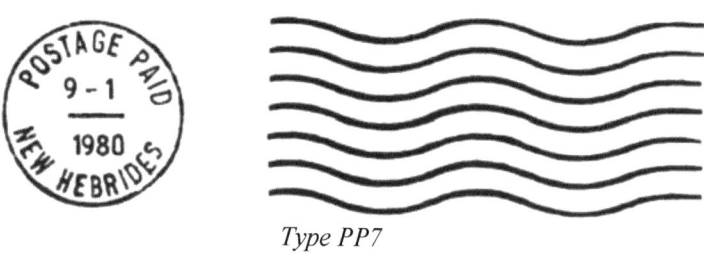

Type PP7

Type PP7. New Hebrides English postage-paid mark. It was introduced in 1979 and used until Independence.

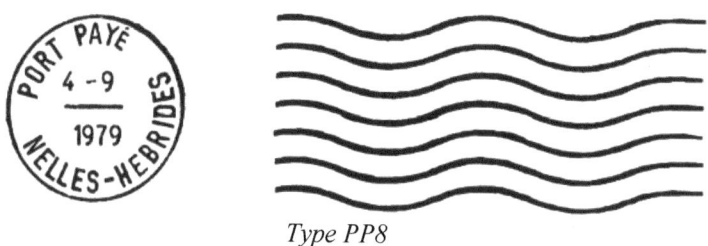

Type PP8

Type PP8. New Hebrides French postage-paid mark equivalent of PP7.

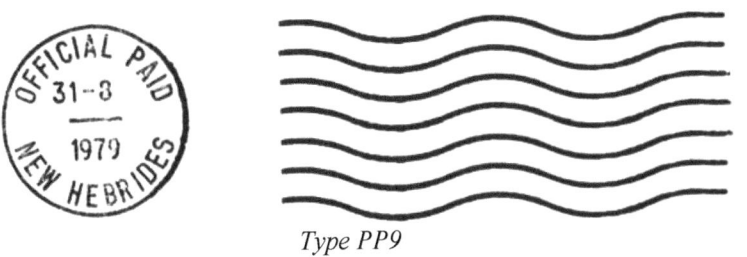

Type PP9

Type PP9. New Hebrides English official-mail mark. It was introduced in 1979 and used until Independence.

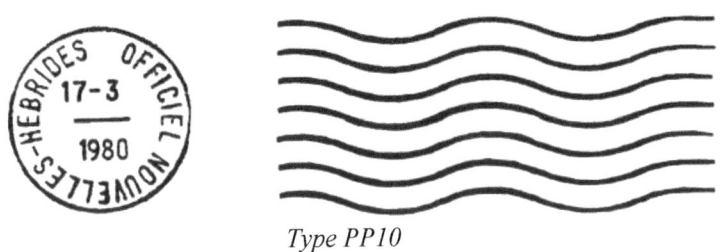

Type PP10

Type PP10. New Hebrides French official-mail mark equivalent of PP9.

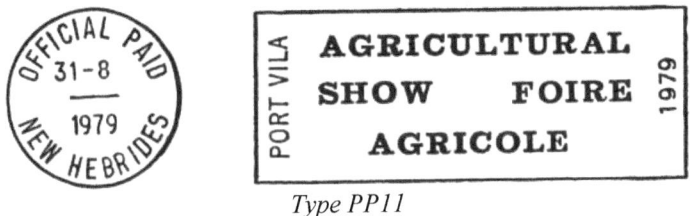

Type PP11

Type PP11. New Hebrides English official-mail mark with the slogan for the Agricultural Show. This was used during August 1979 and is the only example of a postage-paid mark with a slogan that we have seen.

Scarcity. The postage-paid marks appear to be in the common category (see page 104). However, PP1 is rare and PP11 scarce.

New Hebrides Postal History

SECTION C

REGISTRATION CACHETS / LABELS

A group of men in a canoe, New Hebrides. CFNH / EB postcard series 1 (Number 119), published circa 1925.

8. REGISTRATION CACHETS / LABELS (1903-1950)

All of the registration cachets and labels that were used in the New Hebrides and are listed here include the letter 'R' in their design. We have designated these as NR types to distinguish them from previous listings that used the designation R types (see Appendix IV).

The NSW postal agency did not employ cachets for registered mail, but simply applied a manuscript registration number. The first registration cachets (NR1A and NR1B) were introduced by the NC postal agency and were used with a manuscript registration number elsewhere on the cover. This lasted until the opening of the Condominium Post Office in 1908. In our opinion the inter-island vessels did not offer a registered mail service again until the early 1920s (when NR1A was again employed). The few maritime registered covers that are known from 1909 to 1920 appear to be 'philatelic' and have a NR1C mark, which presumably was added after the mail was landed in Port Vila.

From 1908 to 1923 a boxed 'R' cachet (NR1) was the only type used, with the registration number added in manuscript elsewhere on the cover. From 1923 to 1950 either cachets or labels were used (Types NR2 – NR19) with a manuscript (or occasionally typewritten) registration number added to a cachet, and either a manuscript or printed number added to a label. The rationale for using either a cachet or a label is unclear.

Generally, all registration cachets were applied using black ink (Figure 84A), but there were times when other coloured inks were employed. For example, blue (Figure 84B), purple (Figure 84C) and red-brown (Figure 84D). This is an area that would benefit from specialist study.

Figure 84A   *Figure 84B*   *Figure 84C*   *Figure 84D*

Type NR1A   *Type NR1B*   *Type NR1C*

Type NR1. New Hebrides boxed 'R' cachet consisting of an octagonal box. The cachet was accompanied by a manuscript registration number elsewhere on the cover.

Type NR1A (15.5mm high x 13mm wide) can be distinguished from NR1C by the indistinct horizontal line at the top of the 'R' (Figure 85A). It is known used in 1905 (but may have been in use from 1903) and was replaced the following year by NR1B. At a later date it was brought back into service and is known on covers posted on the Messageries Maritime vessels between 1920 and 1928. It was replaced by NR8 in 1929.

Type NR1B can be distinguished from NR1A and NR1C, because it has a thin 'R' and the inner surface at the top right of the 'R' is curved (Figure 85B). The box is also squarer (14mm high x 13mm wide) rather than octagonal. It replaced NR1A in 1906 and was used until 1908.

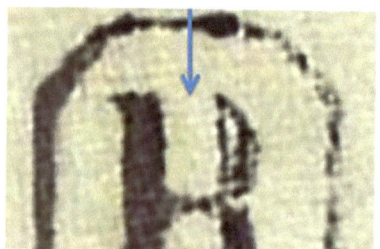 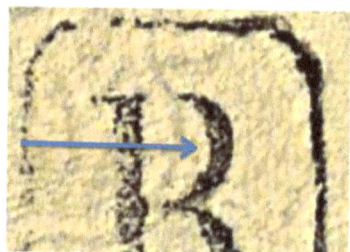

Figure 85A   *Figure 85B*

Type NR1C (15.5 mm high x 13mm wide) was the only registration cachet during the early years of the Condominium postal service. It was based at the Port Vila post office and used from 1908 until 1924, though it is also known on a few covers during 1929 to 1932. It is possible that this cachet was also used on maritime mail landed at Port Vila from 1909 to 1920.

NR1C was replaced by the Vila English NR3 and Port Vila French NR4 cachets in 1924. These were in turn replaced by NR5 and NR6 in 1926. The use of English Vila cachets was phased out during the 1930s and labels used in their place. The registration labels were exclusively printed as Vila (not Port Vila) until 1949. NR6 was replaced with the NR9 cachet in 1931, which continued in use until 1950.

It is unclear what criteria were used in deciding whether a cachet (either English or French) or a label should be used on registered mail. Their use may have been random.

   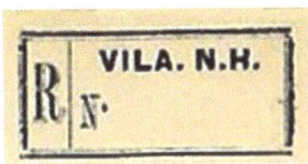

Type NR2A   *Type NR2B*

Type NR2. Vila English registration label. This label can be distinguished from NR10 because it has a dot after VILA , but no hyphen before 'H'.

Type NR2A measured 38mm wide x 15mm high and has a solid 'R'. There is no French equivalent. It is known used from 1923 to 1925.

Type NR2B measured 34mm wide x 16mm high, has a shaded and much smaller 'R'. It is known used from the mid 1920s to 1930.

Type NR3

Type NR3. Vila English registration cachet, measuring 42mm wide x 16mm high with a gothic 'R'. It is known used from July 1924 until March 1925, when it was replaced by NR5.

Type NR4

Type NR4. Port-Vila French registration cachet, measuring 49mm wide x 16mm high, with a gothic 'R', which is the French equivalent of NR3. It is known used from November 1924 until February 1926.

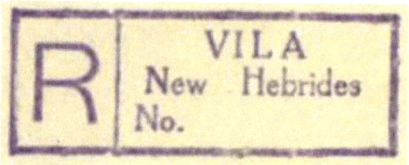

Type NR5

Type NR5. Vila English registration cachet, measuring 40mm wide x 14mm high with a sans serif 'R'. It replaced Type NR3 in 1926 and was mainly used until 1930, though covers with this cachet are known as late as March 1938. Computer analysis indicates that there were two handstamps, but the differences are too insignificant to designate them subtypes. One may have been a metal device (which is scarce) and the other rubber (and often smudged). This was the last English registration cachet used by the Port Vila Post Office.

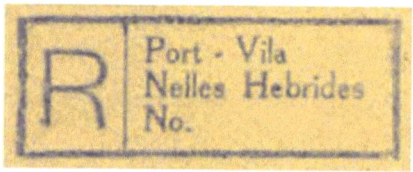

Type NR6

Type NR6. Port-Vila French registration cachet, measuring 40mm wide x 14mm high with a sans serif 'R', which is the French equivalent of NR5. Computer analysis indicates that there were two hand-stamps, but the differences are too insignificant to designate them subtypes. One may have been a metal device (which gave a clear impression) and the other rubber (which is uncommon). It replaced Type NR4 in 1926 and was used until 1930, when it was replaced by NR9.

Type NR7A *Type NR7B*

Type NR7. Provisional Vila registration label, which was probably printed locally and included a printed registration number.

Type NR7A has closely spaced VILA. It was used sporadically from 1929 to 1939, presumably when stocks of the usual labels were depleted.

Type NR7B has wider spaced VILA. It is known used from 1943 to 1949. This label is also known used as a numbering device, in conjunction with NR18 on Santo registered covers in the mid-1940s.

Type NR8

Type NR8. Sce Maritimes registration cachet, measuring 45mm wide by 17mm high. It was carried on S.S. La Perouse and replaced NR1A. It is known from 1929 to 1930, after which it was replaced by NR11A.

Type NR9

Type NR9. Port-Vila French registration cachet, measuring 41mm wide x 12mm high. It is well known for the misspelt VILLA. It replaced NR6 in 1931 and was used until 1950.

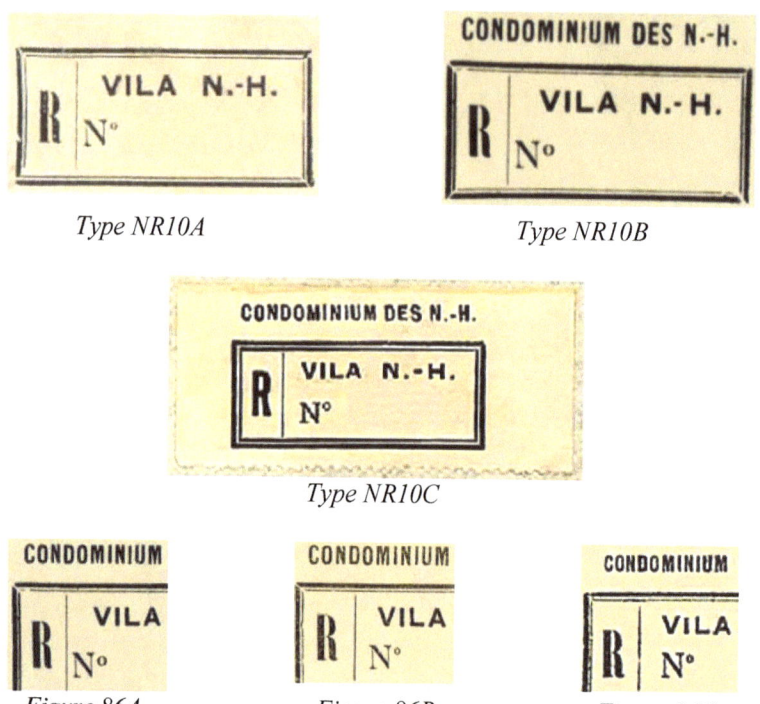

Type NR10A   *Type NR10B*

Type NR10C

Figure 86A   *Figure 86B*   *Figure 86C*

Type NR10. Vila registration label. This label can be distinguished from NR2 as there is no dot after VILA, but there is a hyphen before 'H'.

Type NR10A. The frame measures 36mm x 16mm. It is distinguished from NR10B by the lack of the 'CONDOMINIUM DES N. –H.' inscription. It was used from 1931 to 1933.

Type NR10B. The frame measures 36mm x 16mm. It is distinguished from NR10A by the 'CONDOMINIUM DES N. -H.' inscription. Three variants are known with the 'N°' printed at different positions relative to the 'V' of VILA (Figures 86A – 86C). NR10B was used from 1933 to 1938.

Type NR10C. The frame measures 36mm x 15mm and is distinguished from NR10B by the sans-serif 'R'. It replaced NR10B in 1938 and was used until 1944.

Type NR11A

Type NR11B

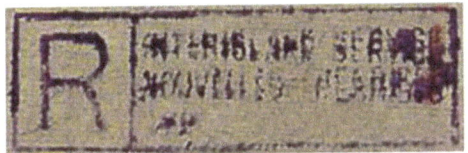
Type NR11C

Type NR11. Interisland service registration cachet. Although the differences between these cachets are minor, we list them as separate subtypes, because the hand-stamps were carried by different interisland ships. These were used from 1932 to 1937.

Type NR11A. This cachet has smaller lettering than NR11B, measuring 41mm wide x 13mm high, and was used on S.S. La Perouse from 1932 to 1935.

Type NR11B. This cachet has larger lettering than NR11A, measuring 41mm wide x 14mm high, and was used on S.S. Pierre Loti from 1936 to 1937.

Type NR11C. This cachet differs from NR11A and NR11B in that 'H' of Hebrides is to the right of 'D' of interisland. It measured 41mm wide x 13mm high and was used on S.S. Morinda from 1936 to 1937.

Type NR12

Type NR12. Service maritime registration cachet, measuring 43mm wide x 10mm high. It was located on S.S. Bucephale and used from 1934 to 1937.

Type NR13

Type NR13. S.S. Pierre Loti registration label. This is NR7A, with VILA crossed out and PIERRE LOTI hand-stamped. It was used during 1937 and then replaced by NR14.

Type NR14

Type NR14. Inter-isles registration cachet, measuring 41mm wide x 12mm high. It was located on S.S. Pierre Loti and used from 1938 to 1940.

Type NR15

Type NR15. Inter-island registration cachet, measuring 40mm wide x 12mm high. This was located on S.S. Morinda and used from 1938 to 1947.

Type NR16

Type NR16. British Administration registration cachet, measuring 41mm wide x 12mm high. It had H.B.M.R.C. (His Britannic Majesty's Resident Commissioner) and the registration number typed onto the cachet and is known used on official stampless mail in 1938.

Type NR17

Type NR17. Santo registration label. This is NR7A with VILA crossed out and SANTO added in manuscript. It was first used as a registration label in 1940, but in 1941 its function changed to a numbering device that was used in conjunction with NR18. This use continued until 1942.

Type NR18

Type NR18. Santo French registration cachet, measuring 41mm wide x 12mm high. It was used from 1941 to 1952, though a premature use on a 1937 maritime (possibly 'philatelic') cover is known. Despite previous reports we know of no English equivalent cachet.

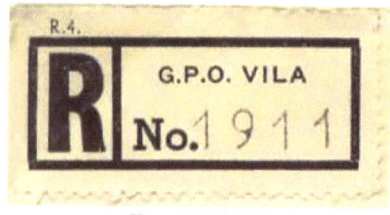 

Type NR19A   *Type NR19B*

Type NR19. Vila R4 registration label with a black-frame (measuring 38mm wide x 15mm high) and 'R4' above top left corner of frame. A pagination machine entered the registration number on the label. These were probably provisional labels, which were used during a temporary shortage of the blue-frame R5 labels.

Type NR19A. G.P.O. VILA was printed on the label and used in 1949.

Type NR19B. VILA was hand-stamped on the label and used in 1950.

Scarcity. Table 19 lists the relative scarcity of the registration cachets and labels used during the 1903 to 1950 period.

Table 19. Scarcity of New Hebrides NR registration cachets / labels (1903-1950)

Scarcity	PM Types
Rare	NR11A, NR13, NR16
Scarce	NR1A, NR1B, NR8, NR11B, NR11C
Uncommon	NR2B, NR12, NR14, NR15, NR19B
Common	All other cachets / labels

8. BLUE-FRAME REGISTRATION LABELS (1949-1980)

Introduction

From 1949 to 1980 registered mail had a label incorporating the letter 'R' within a blue-frame (measuring 38mm wide x 14mm high). There were three basic designs for these labels, which we designate R5 (Figure 87A), R6 (Figure 87B) and R7 (Figure 87C). Each label also had a four-figure registration number added.

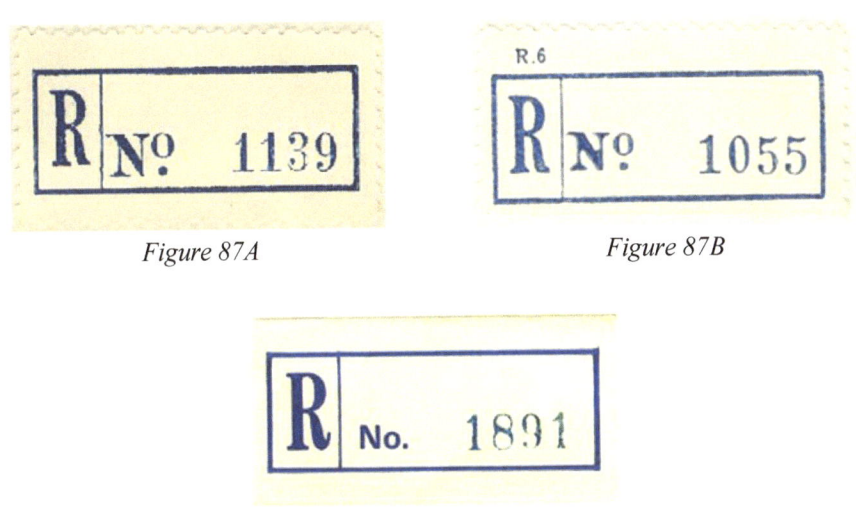

Figure 87A   Figure 87B

Figure 87C

The first label design had no inscription, but we refer to it as the R5 label (Figure 87A) as its period of use was between that of the R4 (NR19) and R6 labels. Although the R6 label replaced it from the early 1960s, it appears that the R5 label was reintroduced for use by certain small post offices that were established during the 1970s. The R6 label had 'R6' printed above the top left corner of the frame (Figure 87B). The R7 label replaced it in 1973. The R7 label differs from the R5 label by its sans serif 'No' (Figure 87C). Although this label has no R7 designation, we refer to it as the R7 label because it was used after the R6 label was gradually phased out (Table 20).

The R5 and R6 labels are known with the name of the post office printed on the label. However, all three types are also known as blank labels onto which the post office name was added by some other method.

The classification of these labels is not straightforward, as many variants are known. This listing is in our opinion the most rational. Each post office is listed as a separate type (as with the PM26 – PM45 postmarks) and in chronological order according to the first appearance of their blue-frame labels. The different labels (either with a printed post office name or blank) are listed as subtypes. In addition we also include the 1957 Port Vila provisional label (NR20B) as a subtype. Variants of the blank labels that are associated with differences in their printings, methods of adding the post office name, or the font of the registration numbering, are a matter for specialist study and are outside the scope of this classification.

Table 20. The periods of use of blue frame registration labels by New Hebrides post offices (1949-1980).

POST OFFICE	TYPE	REGISTRATION LABEL	DATES OF USE
Port Vila	NR20	R5	1949-1960
		R6	1960-1973
		R7	1973-1980
Santo	NR21	R5	1952-1965
		R6	1965-1974
		R7	1973-1980
Lamap	NR23	R5	1958-1963
		R6	1963-1978
		R7	1973-1978
Forari	NR22	R5	1962-1963
		R6	1963-1969
Tanna	NR24	R6	1963-1976
		R7	1974-1980
Longana	NR25	R6*	1970-1978
Melsisi	NR26	R5*	1972-1978
Norsup	NR27	R5	1975-1980
		R7	1975-1980
Tongoa	NR28	R5	1976-1980
		R7	1976-1980
Lolowai	NR29	R5*	1978-1980

* At the time of writing, we have not seen R7 labels from these post offices, but they may exist and would have been used during these periods.

Classification of blue-frame labels

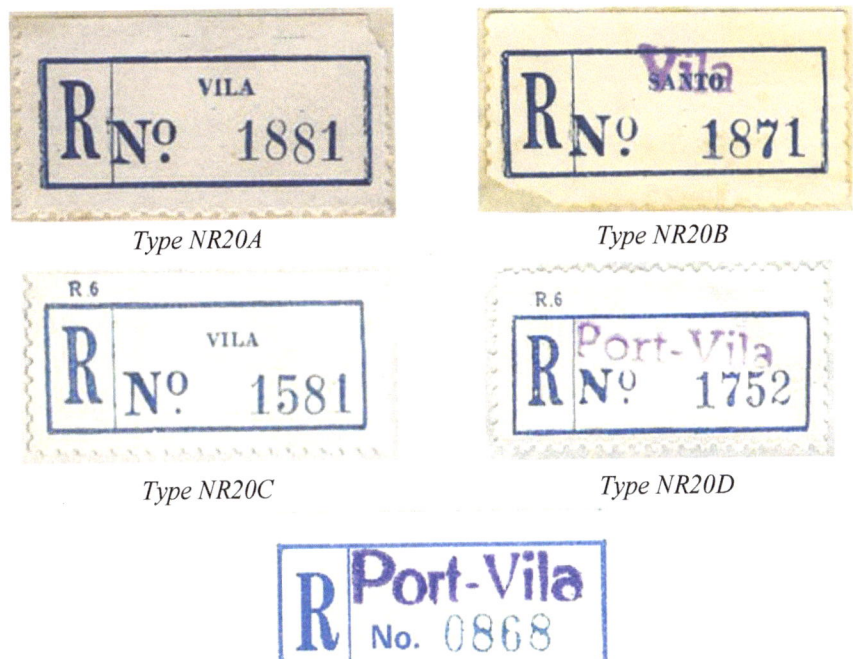

Type NR20A

Type NR20B

Type NR20C

Type NR20D

Type NR20E

Type NR20. Port Vila blue-frame registration label.

Type NR20A. VILA printed R5 label.

Type NR20B. Vila hand-stamped over SANTO of NR21A. This was a provisional label that was used during 1957, when stocks of NR20A had become temporarily depleted.

Type NR20C. VILA printed R6 label.

Type NR20D. Port Vila blank R6 label. The name (Vila or Port Vila) was added by a hand-stamp, of which there are several variants.

Type NR20E. Port Vila blank R7 label. The name (Vila or Port Vila) was added by either a hand-stamp (several variants) or in manuscript. There are also several font variants of the registration number.

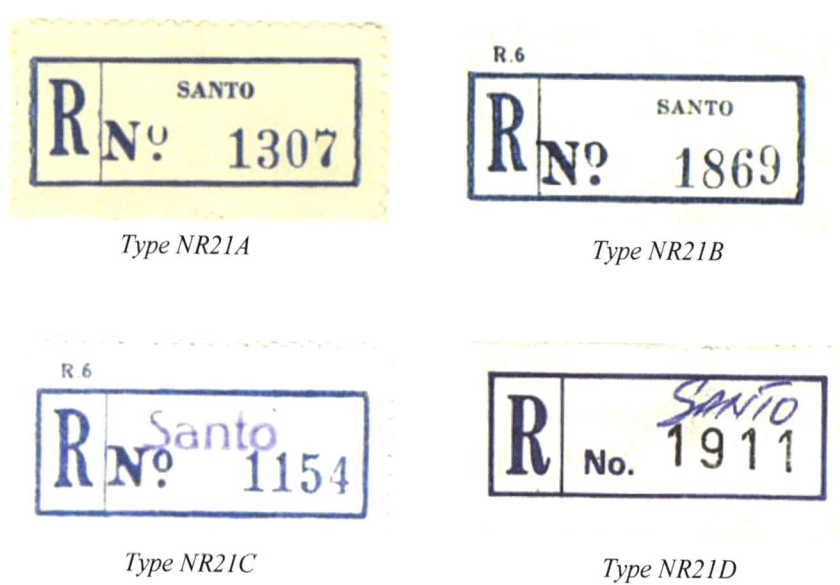

Type NR21A *Type NR21B*

Type NR21C *Type NR21D*

Type NR21. Santo blue-frame registration label.

Type NR21A. SANTO printed R5 label.

Type NR21B. SANTO printed R6 label.

Type NR21C. Santo blank R6 label. The name was added by a hand-stamp, of which there are several variants.

Type NR21D. Santo blank R7 label. The name was added either by a hand-stamp (several variants) or in manuscript. There are also several font variants of the registration number.

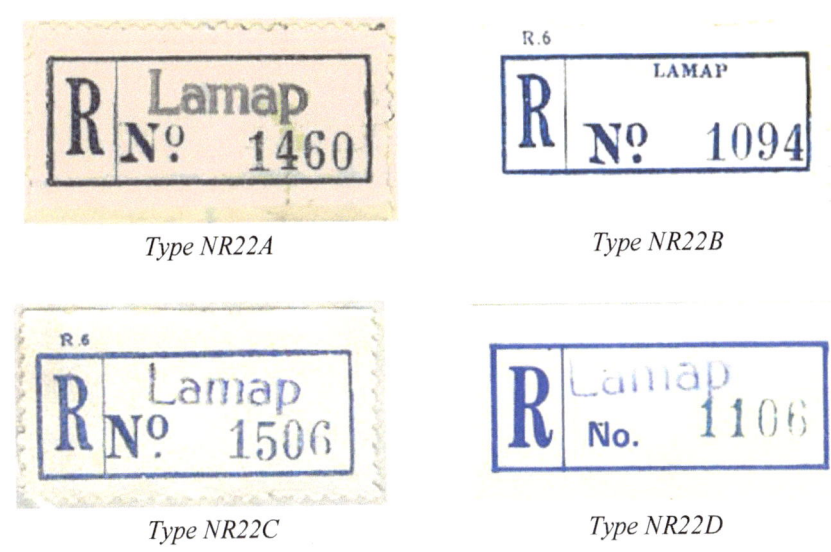

Type NR22A   Type NR22B

Type NR22C   Type NR22D

Type NR22. Lamap blue-frame registration label.

Type NR22A. Lamap blank R5 registration label. Lamap was added by a hand-stamp. It was used from the opening of the post office in 1958 until 1963.

Type NR22B. Lamap printed R6 registration label. It replaced NR23A in 1963 and was used until the early 1970s.

Type NR22C. Lamap blank R6 registration label. Lamap was added by a hand-stamp. It was used from the mid-1970s until the post office closed in 1978.

Type NR22D. Lamap blank R7 registration label. Lamap was added by either a hand-stamp (several variants) or in manuscript. It was used from the mid 1970s until the post office closed in 1978.

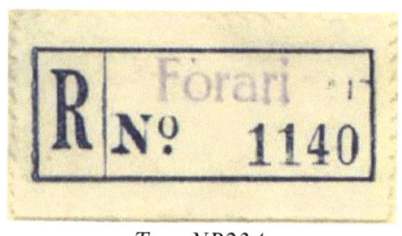 

Type NR23A   *Type NR23B*

Type NR23. Forari blue-frame registration label.

Type NR23A. Forari blank R5 registration label. Forari was added by a hand-stamp. It was used from the opening of the post office in 1962 until early in 1963.

Type NR23B. Forari printed R6 registration label. It replaced NR22A and was used until 1969 when the post office closed.

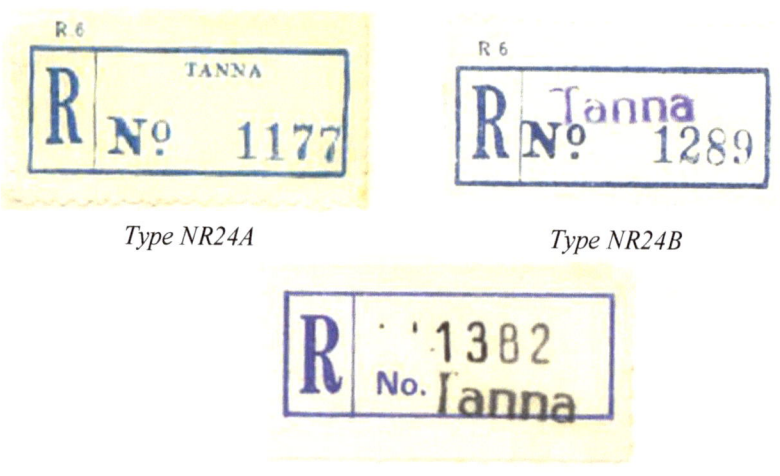

Type NR24C

Type NR24. Tanna blue-frame registration label.

Type NR24A. Tanna printed R6 registration label.
Type NR24B. Tanna blank R6 registration label. The name was added by either a hand-stamp (several variants) or in manuscript.
Type NR24C. Tanna blank R7 registration label. The name was added by a hand-stamp, of which there are several variants.

Type NR25

Type NR25. Longana blue-frame blank R6 registration label. LONGANA was added by either a boxed hand-stamp or in manuscript. We have never seen R7 labels used at Longana, but if they exist then the R5 label should be designated NR25A and the R7 label as NR25B.

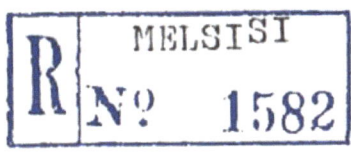

Type NR26

Type NR26. Melsisi blue-frame blank R5 registration label. MELSISI was added either typewritten or in manuscript. We have never seen R7 labels used at Melsisi, but if they exist then the R5 label should be designated NR26A and the R7 label as NR26B.

Type NR27A   *Type NR27B*

Type NR27. Norsup blue-frame registration label.

Type NR27A. Norsup blank R5 registration label. NORSUP was added either typewritten or in manuscript.

Type NR27B. Norsup blank R7 registration label. NORSUP was added in manuscript.

Type NR28A

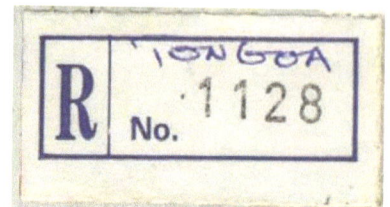
Type NR28B

Type NR28. Tongoa blue-frame registration label.

Type NR28A. Tongoa blank R5 registration label. Tongoa was added either typewritten or in manuscript.

Type NR28B. Tongoa blank R7 registration label. TONGOA was added in manuscript.

Type NR29

Type NR29. Lolowai blue-frame blank R5 registration label. LOLOWAI was added either typewritten or in manuscript. We have never seen R7 labels used at Lolowai, but if they exist then the R5 label should be designated NR29A and the R7 label as NR29B.

Scarcity. As the blue frame registration labels were frequently used on 'philatelic' mail they can all be regarded as common. The use of these labels on commercial mail from the smaller post offices is much scarcer.

Variants of blue-frame labels

During the 30 years that these labels were in use many variants occurred. This has resulted in a complex picture. The R6 and R7 labels are known with two distinctive printings. In addition to the R5 and R6 labels that included a printed post office name, all three labels were used as blank labels onto which the post office name was added in various ways (typewritten, hand-stamped, or in manuscript). Several variants of the hand-stamps exist and there are differences in the ink colour that was used in their application. There are also several variants in the font used for registration numbers on the R7 labels. This is an interesting area that would benefit from specialist study.

Two printings of the R6 label can be distinguished. One with the smaller 'No' (Figure 88A) is known used from 1960 until 1973. The variant with the larger 'No' (Figure 88B) is known used from 1968 until 1971.

Figure 88A

Figure 88B

Two printings of the R7 can be distinguished by the thinner (Figure 89A) or thicker lettering (Figure 89B). The variant with thinner lettering was used throughout the 1972 to 1980 period, but the use of the thicker lettering variant appears to have been restricted to between 1975 and 1976.

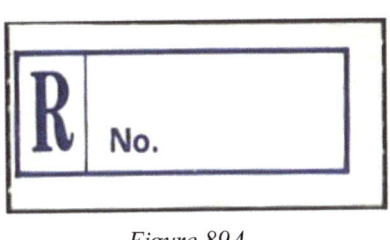
Figure 89A

Figure 89B

The R7 registration labels that were used by the Philatelic Bureau in Port Vila often had a red 'P' added in manuscript (Figure 90).

Figure 90

The blank labels had the name of the post office added. This could be either typewritten (Figure 91A), hand-stamped (Figure 91B) or in manuscript (Figure 91C).

Figure 91A

Figure 91B   Figure 91C

The hand-stamps were applied using inks of various shades of blue / purple (Figure 92A), or in black (Figure 92B). An unauthorized red hand-stamp is known (see PU17).

Figure 92A

Figure 92B

The hand-stamps varied considerably in their format. Examples are known with the post office name in capital letters only (Figure 93A) or capital and lower case letters (Figure 93B). The size and font of the lettering used in the hand-stamps also varied (for example Figures 93C and 93D).

Figure 93A

Figure 93B

Figure 93C

Figure 93D

The registration number on the labels always consisted of four figures. It appears that a pagination machine was used to add a number to the R5 (Figure 94A), R6 (Figure 94B) and initially R7 (Figure 94C) labels.

Figure 94A

Figure 94B

Figure 94C

During the mid to late 1970s, alternate procedures were introduced to add a registration number to the R7 labels. These produced a number variants with different fonts (for example Figures 95A - 95D), of which at least eight different variants are known.

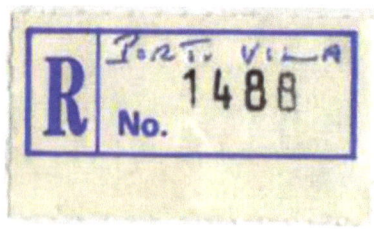

Figure 95A

Figure 95B

Figure 95C

Figure 95D

152

APPENDICES

A group of people with their canoes on a beach in Malekula, New Hebrides. CFNH / EB postcard series 2, Format A (Number 2), published circa 1935.

Appendix I. Printed-paper rates

Occasionally covers are encountered that have a lower postage than the prevailing letter rate, but which have not attracted a postage due charge (Figures 96 and 97). These covers probably included printed papers and therefore were charged at the printed-paper rate.

Table 21 summarises the printed-paper rates that were used during the different periods. From 1927 these were published, but before that time the published information is incomplete and a number of rates have to be inferred from studying postal history. The latter therefore need confirmation.

Table 21. Printed-paper rates.

PERIOD	DESTINATION	RATE
NSW postal agency	All	1d per 4oz
NC postal agency	All	4c per 50g (up to Sept. 1903)
		5c per 50g (from Oct. 1903)
1908-1920	British colonial	1d per 4oz (up to Dec. 1912)
		½d per 4oz (from Dec. 1912)
	French colonial	5c per 50g
	Non-colonial	1d (10c) per 50g
1920-1927	Colonial	1d (10c) per 50g
	Non-colonial	1½d (15c) per 50g
1927-1937	Local	1d (10c) per 50g
	Colonial	1½d (15c) per 50g
	Non-colonial	3d (30c) per 50g
1938 (January – May)	Colonial	3d (30c) per 50g
	Non-colonial	3d (30c) per 50g
1938-1960	Colonial	5gc per 50g (up to 1949)
		10gc per 50g (from 1949)
	Non-colonial	5gc per 50g (up to 1950)
		10gc per 50g (from 1950)
1961-1970	Colonial	10gc per 100g
	Non-colonial	10gc per 50gc
1970-1972	Colonial	15gc per 100g
	Non-colonial	15gc per 50g
1972-1977	Colonial	15gc per 20g
	Non-colonial	20gc per 20g
1977-1980	Local	5FNH per 20g
	Overseas	10FNH per 20g

Figure 96. Cover to Epi, New Hebrides. The 1d stamp, which was cancelled by a Vila PM7A postmark (dated 16th May 1929), paid the local printed-paper rate. The local letter rate at that time was 2d.

Figure 97. Cover posted within Port Vila. The 15gc stamp, which was cancelled by a Port Vila PM30B postmark (dated 28th June 1976), paid the colonial printed-paper rate. The colonial letter rate at that time was 25gc.

Appendix II. Philatelic covers

As we have mentioned previously, there is a considerable amount of postal history material from the New Hebrides that can be classed as 'philatelic'. During the Condominium's history, collectors and dealers have frequently prepared covers and then sent them to the Condominium Post Office under separate cover, so that they could be cancelled and returned to them. The Condominium postal officials were agreeable to these activities and, as long as the stamps paid the required postage, made no objection to cancelling overpaid covers.

On one hand, some of these covers show the correct use of stamps with the appropriate postal rates (for example, some of the Leralle and Meister covers) and we have no problems with those. On the other hand, some covers are purely 'philatelic' fantasies that are worthless (for example, the Schreiber postage due covers). In between these two extremes are many covers that were overpaid, or show an inappropriate use of postmarks etc.

Table 22 is a listing of the most common addressees on these covers and indicates the years that they were most active. This list is not exhaustive, but is provided so that if a collector encounters covers addressed to any of these people, they should exercise caution before acquiring them.

Table 22. Listing of addressees on 'philatelic' covers

ADDRESSEE	PERIOD OF ACTIVITY
Ackland, W.	1920-1924
Ashley, G.C.A.	1921-1925
Baldwin, B.A.	1940-1944
Bayer, S.L.	1941
Belmonte, E.C.	1924-1926
Buess, K.	1910-922
Calder, D.	1897-1898
Clements, W.G.	1909-1914
Cliquet, C.	1909-1913
Conus, E.	1935
Conway, A.	1957
Dorn, P.A.	1951-1955
Guthrie, W.R.	1950-1951
Hambly, J.F.	1897-1941
Jourdain, M.G.	1941-1943

Kiderlen, P.	1909-1926
Kinze, J.	1908-1909
Klinkmüller, G.	1911-1912
Leralle, A.L.	1923-1938
Meister, L.	1920-1932
Merot, J.	1970-1980
Murray, R.H.	1912
Naumann, H.	1912
Nicolini, J.A.	1970-1980
Nickoletich, N.	1920-1924
Queyroy, E.	1949
Reinhard, F.	1912
Rossi, M.	1908
Scott, J.B.E.	1974-1978
Shrieber, L.I.	1951 postage due covers
Stolow	1941
Surroz, L.	1961
Thouvignon, F.	1938-1939
Tubb, J. (pseudonym of J. Hambly)	1940-1941
White, W.A.	1953
Wilson, W.	1911-1938

Appendix III. Unauthorized postmarks

This listing contains postmarks (and a registration label) that were never authorized for use by any recognized postal authority. They include company marks and fakes, which we designate as PU types.

Type PU1

Type PU2

Types PU1 & PU2. ANHCo postmarks.

The ANHCo (see pages 8-9) claimed that Types PU1 and PU2 were needed to cancel its cinderella stamp issues that had been postally used, but in fact their main use was to produce cancel-to-order (CTO) sheets of those cinderellas. Some of the CTO cinderellas are known with 1896 dates (i.e. a year before they were issued) and some examples are known cancelled either in black or purple, but with the same date (i.e. the ANHCo presumably ran out of black ink during those CTO sessions and had to resort to using purple ink). Dates known are from 1896 until the early 1900s. The use of PU1 or PU2 on covers or postcards is 'philatelic'.

Type PU3

Type PU3. Port Vila postmark. This is a 'philatelic' concoction, which was possibly hand-designed. It is known used on the ANHCo cinderellas with a 1897 date

Type PU4A *Type PU4B* *Type PM1*

Type PU4. Forgeries of PM1.

Type PU4A. This is a dangerous forgery and is based on a cliché made from a genuine PM1 postmark. It always looks the same, with over-inking at the top right and a date of 4th September 1897.

Type PU4B. PM1 with single line separators between NEW HEBRIDES and VILA. This is a copy of a pull from the cancel, taken before the Royal Sydney Philatelic Society destroyed it in the 1940s.

Type PU5

Type PU5. SFNH Franceville postmark. This cancel was manufactured by the SFNH group that also printed the SFNH cinderellas (see pages 14-15). It was used on both the SFNH cinderellas and NC stamps (dated from 1903 to 1908), but is a 'philatelic' fantasy.

Type PU6

Type PU6. Port Hanavannah postmark. This is known used on SFNH cinderellas (dated from 1903 to 1908) and is another 'philatelic' fantasy.

New Hebrides Postal History

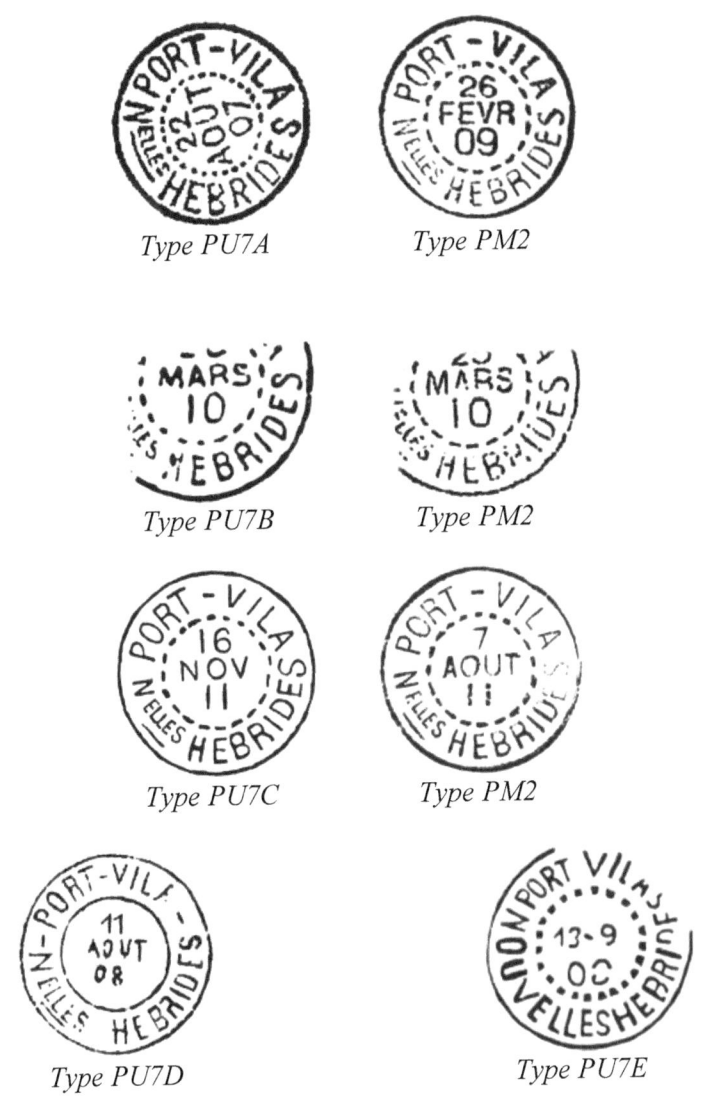

Type PU7. Forgeries of PM2.

Type PU7A is a poor forgery of PM2. Our archive reveals that dozens of postcards with stamps (usually SFNH cinderellas) have been cancelled with this fake. This forgery has the ELLES completely underlined, whereas the genuine postmark has E<u>LL</u>ES.

Type PU7B is known only as a partial postmark on stamps. Its main distinguishing characteristics are that it has too few dashes in the inner circle. MARS is too small and 'S' of HEBRIDES is malformed.

Type PU7C is the so-called Alavoine forgery. Its main characteristic is the malformed 'P'.

Type PU7D is a rather crude forgery with a primitive date block. It is often seen on picture postcards.

Type PU7E is rarely seen and is a poor forgery of PM2 that is easily identified. It is sometimes found on Australian postcards together with forged cancels of other countries.

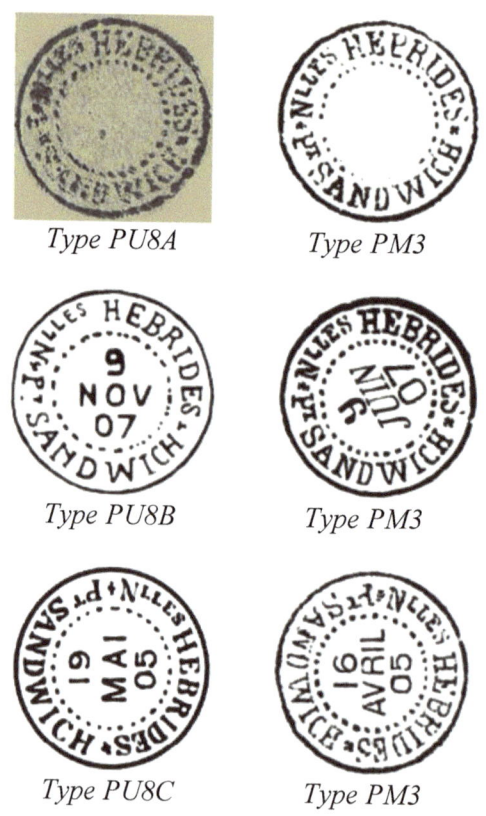

Type PU8A   Type PM3

Type PU8B   Type PM3

Type PU8C   Type PM3

Type PU8. Forgeries of PM3.

Type PU8A is a poor cliché forgery of the missing date block variant of PM3. The genuine missing date block variant is much clearer and distinct.

Type PU8B is a dangerous forgery. It can be distinguished from the genuine postmark because of (a) the 'S' of HEBRIDES has the wrong shape, (b) the 'S' of SANDWICH is too small, (c) the start of SANDWICH is too high on the left side.

Type PU8C is a forgery of PM3 which originates from a description of an exhibit page of the late U.S. collector Stan Jersey. The exhibition drawing was used to make a cliché with the date 19th May 1905. Examples of this forgery are usually found on stamps used on piece.

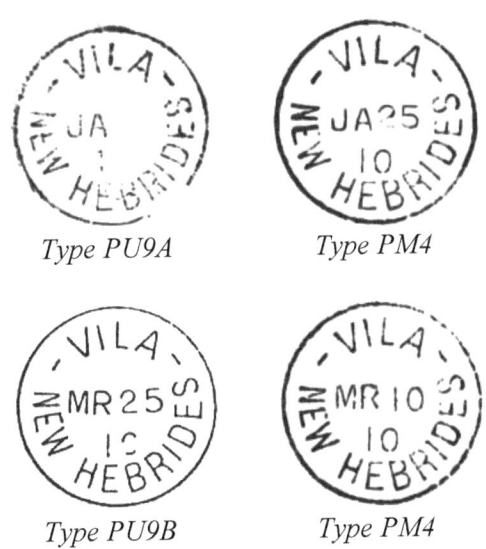

Type PU9A   Type PM4

Type PU9B   Type PM4

Type PU9. Forgeries of PM4.

Type PU9A is known on some documents, but is not common. The 'I' of the year is a different font to the genuine postmark.

Type PU9B is the most dangerous forgery of a New Hebrides postmark and is known as the Madame Joseph forgery after Warboys' book, 'Madame Joseph forged postmarks'. The impression is always very faint and the 'R' of 'MR' is slightly wider than the genuine postmark. It is found with a March date on scarce New Hebrides stamps (mostly low grade copies) and has fooled expert committees. As used examples of these stamps have higher catalogue values, it is probable that the use of PU9B was to enhance the value of unused stamps.

Type PU10   *Type PM8*

Type PU10. A forgery of PM8. It was forged by making a cliché from the Betrand Sinais / Guy Venot Catalogue of Cancellations, page 288. This forgery occurs on large covers with the complete 1925 definitive stamp set, which sometimes bear the imprint, HOSPITAL MARITIME DE L'ORATOIRE.

Type PU11   *Type PM9A*

Type PU11. A forgery of PM9A. It was forged by making a cliché from the Betrand Sinais / Guy Venot Catalogue of Cancellations, page 288. This forgery occurs on large covers with the complete 1925 definitive stamp set, which sometimes bear the imprint, HOSPITAL MARITIME DE L'ORATOIRE.

POSTED AT SEA
NEW-HEBRIDES

Type PU12

Type PU13

Types PU12 & PU13. Leralle paquebot cancels. These cancels are known on covers from 1934 to 1938, almost all of which were addressed to Mr. Leralle, or to one of his pseudonyms. This fact leads us to conclude that they were 'philatelic' concoctions. The genuine New Hebrides paquebot mark was PM12.

Type PU12 is a two line unboxed POSTED AT SEA (84mm x 5mm) NEW-HEBRIDES (57mm x 3mm) cancel. Type PU13 is a boxed straight-line PAQUEBOT cancel, measuring 59mm x 12mm. Other variants with thinner letters, or measuring 50mm x 12mm, have also been reported.

Type PU14A   *Type PU14B*

Type PU14. Vila paquebot cancel. Single circle of diameter 33mm with small date (Type PU10A) or diameter 35mm with large date (Type PU10B). These have dates from the late 1940s to 1950, but we can find no evidence that they are genuine marks. The genuine New Hebrides paquebot cancel was PM12.

PAQUEBOT

Type PU15

Type PU15. Santo paquebot mark, consisting of an unboxed straight PAQUEBOT measuring 26mm by 4mm. It has been reported used in the 1950s, but genuine paquebot covers landed at Santo had their stamps cancelled by dumb cancels (with an adjacent Santo circular date stamp).

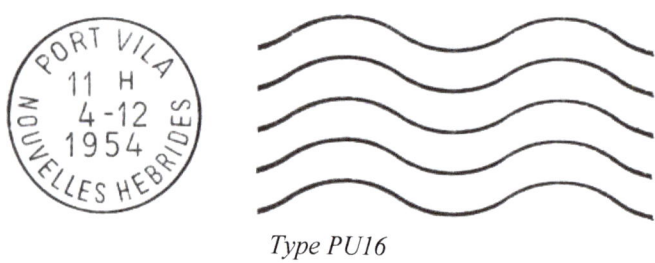

Type PU16

Type PU16. SECAP cancel, consisting of a single circle date stamp (diameter 22mm), which is identical to that of Type PS2, but is distinguished by the five wavy lines. It was probably used in France and applied to publicity postcards sent to medical practitioners in Europe and the USA. These postcards were usually included within other marketing literature, though there is a report that the Condominium Postmaster may have allowed one of the mail shots to be sent through the post from the New Hebrides. The dates known are 4th December 1954, 25th February 1955, 20th August 1966 and 1st September 1966.

Type PU17

Type PU17. Port Vila registration label. This is unlike all other registration labels from the New Hebrides. It is a different size, has a black frame, a different font for the 'R', its registration number is five figures instead of four and the hand-stamp is red. It is known from a 1978 'philatelic' cover, though other examples may exist.

Appendix IV. Comparison with previous studies

Our postmark and registration cachets / label listings are shown in Tables 23 - 27 with the equivalent listings from the three most commonly cited studies.

A - Hals, N. & Collas, P. (1967) The New Hebrides Postal History and their Stamps. The Collectors Club Inc, New York.

B - Phillips, P., Crompton, J. & Holland, B. (1995) New Hebrides Cancellation Study 1892-1980. Pacific Islands Study Circle of Great Britain.

C - Proud, E.B. (2006) The Postal History of the Gilbert and Ellis Islands and New Hebrides. Proud Publications Ltd, Heathfield.

In addition to the above three studies, we are also aware of the following publications.

Hals, N. & Crompton, J. (1980s) New Hebrides cancellation study and listing of registration cachets and labels. Pacific Islands Study Circle of Great Britain.

Sinais, B. & Venot, G. (1989) Catalogue des obliterations des colonies Francaises, I. Les Possessions du Pacifique. Éditions Bertrand Sinais.

Merot, J. (2000) Nouvelles Hébrides oblitérations sur courriers, Bull. Col. Fra. Hors Series, 9A - 13A.

Table 23. Comparison of postmarks authorized for regular use (PM types) with previous studies.

PM Types	A	B	C
1	1, 1a, 6	1, 1A, 6	NSW agency D1
2	5, 5a, 5b	5, 5A	NC agency D2 Vila D2
3	4, 4a	4	Maritime D1 Interisland D1
4	7, 7a, 7b	7, 7A, 7B	Vila D3
5A	40	83, (86)	Interisland D3
5B	42	85	-
5C	41	84	-
6	8	8, 8A	Vila D4, D5
7A	9, 18	9, 9A, 9B	Vila D6
7B	10	10, 10A	Vila D8
7C	12	12	Vila D9
7D	13	13, 13A	Vila D10
8	44	87	Interisland D5
9A	-	88	Interisland D7
9B	47	90	Interisland D8, D11
10	49	93	Interisland D6
11A	11	11	Vila D11
11B	15	14	Vila D12
12A	46	89	-
12B	46	89	Vila SL4
13	48	91	Interisland D4
14	-	94	Interisland D9
15	14	36	Santo D1
16	16, 17	37, 38	Santo D2, D3
17	52	97	Vila SL6
18A	19	16	Vila D15
18B	-	16A	-
19A	21	17, 17A	Vila D13
19B	23	18	Vila D14
20	20	39	Santo D6
21	-	40, 40A	Santo D4, D5
22	-	24	Vila M3
23	33	23	Vila M4
24	-	44	Santo M1

25	-	43	Santo M2
26A	32	59	Lamap D2
26B	31	60	Lamap D3
27A	-	58	Lamap D1
27B	-	61	Lamap D4
28A	28	42	Santo D7
28B	-	47	Santo D11
28C	-	50	Santo D13
29A	27	41	Santo D8
29B	-	48	Santo D12
29C	-	49	Santo D14
30A	30	22	Vila D16, D17
30B	-	26	Vila D18, D19
30C	-	29	Vila D20, D21, D22
31A	29	21	Vila D23
31B	-	27	Vila D24, D25
31C	-	28	Vila D26, D27, D28
32A	-	56	Forari D1
33A	38	55, 57	Forari D2
34A	-	73	Tanna D1
34B	-	75	Tanna D3
34C	-	77	Tanna D5
35A	-	74	Tanna D2
35B	-	76	Tanna D4
35C	-	78	Tanna D6
36B	-	65	Longana D1
37B	-	66	Longana D2
38B	-	67	Melsisi D3
39B	-	68	Melsisi D4
40B	-	69	Norsup D1
40C	-	72	Norsup D3
41B	-	70	Norsup D2
41C	-	71	Norsup D4
42C	-	62	Lolowai D1
43C	-	63	Lolowai D2
44C	-	81	Tongoa D3
45C	-	82	Tongoa D4
46	-	45	Santo D9
47	-	46	Santo D10
48	-	102	Vila SL7
49	-	79	Tongoa D1

50	-	80	Tongoa D2
51	-	32	Vila M5
52	-	33	Vila M6
53	-	52	Santo M3
54	-	51	Santo M4
55	-	30	Vila M7
56	-	31	Vila M8

Figure 98. Postcard to France. The 1½d (15c) stamps, which were cancelled by a Vila Type PM7A postmark (dated 6th December 1927), paid the colonial (no message) postcard rate. See page 33.

(We discovered this card after the book went to press)

Table 24. Comparison of special use postmarks (PS types) with previous studies.

PS Types	A	B	C
1	-	E105	Vila M1
2	-	F106	Vila M2
3A	-	E107	Vila HS1
3B	-	E109, E111, E113, E115, E119,	Vila HS3
3C	-	E117, E121, E124, E128, E130, E132, E136, E140, E142, E144, E146, E150, E152, E156, E158, E160, E164, E176, E178, E180, E182, E184, E186, E188, E190, E192	Vila HS5, HS7, HS13, HS17, HS21, HS35, HS37, HS39,
3D	-	E194, E196, E198, E200, E204, E206, E208, E210, E212, E214	Vila HS41
4A	-	F108	Vila HS2
4B	-	F110, F112, F114, F116, F120	Vila HS4
4C	-	F118, F122, F123, F125, F127, F129, F131, F133, F137, F141, F143, F145, F147, F151, F153, F157, F159, F161, F165, F177, F179, F181, F183, F185, F187, F189, F191, F193	Vila HS6, HS8, HS14, HS18, HS22, HS36, HS38, HS40
4D	-	F195, F197, F199, F201, F205, F207, F209, F211, F213, F215	Vila HS42
5A	-	E113, E119, E124	Santo HS1
5C	-	E126, E128, E130, E132, E136, E140, E146, E150, E152, E156, E158, E160	Santo HS3, HS5, HS11, HS13HS17, HS21, HS23
6A	-	F114, F120, F123, F125	Santo HS2
6C	-	F127, F129, F131, F133, F137, F141, F147, F151, F153, F157, F159, F161	Santo HS4, HS6, HS12, HS14, HS18, HS22, HS24
7	-	E134	Santo HS7

8	-	F135	Santo HS8
9	-	E134	Vila HS9
10	-	F135	Vila HS10
11	-	E138	Santo HS9
12	-	F139	Santo HS10
13	-	E138	Vila HS11
14	-	F139	Vila HS12
15	-	E148	Santo HS15
16	-	F149	Santo HS16
17	-	E148	Vila HS15
18	-	F149	Vila HS16
19	-	E154	Santo HS19
20	-	F155	Santo HS20
21	-	E154	Vila HS19
22	-	F155	Vila HS20
23	-	E162	Santo HS25
24	-	F163	Santo HS26
25	-	E162	Vila HS23
26	-	F163	Vila HS24
27	-	E166	Santo HS27
28	-	F167	Santo HS28
29	-	E166	Vila HS25
30	-	F167	Vila HS26
31	-	E168	Vila HS27
32	-	F169	Vila HS28
33	-	E170	Vila HS29
34	-	F171	Vila HS30
35	-	E172	Vila HS31
36	-	F173	Vila HS32
37	-	E174	Vila HS33
38	-	F175	Vila HS34
39	-	E202	Vila HS43
40	-	F203	Vila HS44
41	-	224	Vila M7 state 2
42	-	225	Vila M8 state 2
43	-	226	Vila M7 state 3
44	-	227	Vila M8 state 3
45	-	228	Vila M7 state 4
46	-	229	Vila M8 state 4

Table 25. Comparison of postage-paid postmarks (PP types) with previous studies.

PP Types	A	B	C
1	-	-	-
2A	-	25	Vila PD3
2B	-	25A	Vila PD4
2C	-	25B	Vila PD5
3	-	35	Vila PD6
4	-	34	-
5	-	217, 218	-
6	-	219	-
7	-	223	Vila PD8
8	-	221	Vila PD9
9	-	222	Vila OPD6
10	-	220	Vila OPD7
11	-	-	-

Table 26. Comparison of registration cachets / labels (NR types) with previous studies.

NR Types	A	B	C
1A	-	-	-
1B	-	-	Travelling Post R1
1C	1	R1, R1A, R54	Vila R1 Interisland R1
2A	2	R2	-
2B	-	-	-
3	4	R4	Vila R3
4	3	R3	Vila R4
5	6, 7	R6, R7	Vila R5
6	-	R5, R9	Vila R6
7A	20	R10	-
7B	-	R14	-
8	-	-	-
9	8	R8	Vila R7
10A	12	R11B	-
10B	-	R11C	-
10C	-	R11	-
11A	9	-	-
11B	-	R55	Interisland R4
11C	-	R55A	-
12	-	R57	Interisland R2
13	-	-	-
14	-	R58	Interisland R3
15	-	R56	Interisland R5
16	-	-	-
17	-	R14A, R34	-
18	-	R31	Santo R1
19A	21	R15	-
19B	22	R16	-
20A	17, 24	R12	-
20B	-	R12A	-
20C	-	R18, R19	-
20D	-	R20, R20A, R21	-
20E	-	R22, R23, R24, R24A, R25, R26, R27, R28, R29, R30	-
21A	18	R33	-

21B	-	R35	-
21C	-	R36	-
21D	-	R37, R38, 3R8A	-
22A	25	R41	-
22B	-	R42	-
22C	-	R43	-
22D	-	-	-
23A	-	R39	-
23B	-	R40	-
24A	-	R50	-
24B	-	R51	-
24C	-	R52	-
25	-	R45	-
26	-	R46, R47	-
27A	-	R48	-
27B	-	R49	-
28A	-	-	-
28B		R53	
29	-	R44	-
			-
*	23	R17	Vila R12
**	-	R13, R32	-

* Previous studies have reported a 'CHARGE' hand stamp on two 1927 covers. It is unclear what function this served, but as it has no letter 'R' incorporated into its design, it is not included in our listing.

** The PISC study included unillustrated reports of an English Santo cachet (R32) and a R5 label with a Vila hand stamp (R13), but we have never seen these and do not think they exist.

Table 27. Comparison of unauthorized postmarks (PU types) with previous studies

PU Types	A	B	C
1	2	2	-
2	3	3	-
3	-	-	-
4A	-	1EU	-
4B	1U	1BU	-
5	11U	-	-
6	-	-	-
7A	-	-	-
7B	-	-	-
7C	9U	5CU, 5DU	-
7D	-	-	-
7E	-	-	-
8A	-	4BU	-
8B	-	4AU	-
8C	-	-	-
9A	-	-	-
9B	-	-	-
10	-	-	-
11	-	-	-
12	-	104	Vila SL2
13	17U	98, 99, 100U	Vila SL3
14A	16U	95	Vila SL5
14B	51	96U	-
15	-	103	Santo SL2
16	-	20	-
17	-	R30A	-
*	7U, 12U, 13U, 14U, 15U	1CU, 1DU, 11AU, 27AU, 92U	-
**	-	13BU	-

* We have never seen examples of these faked postmarks.

** This is a genuine postmark (PM7D), but in purple and dated 14th August 1945. It was used on cancel-to-order sheets of 1938 definitive and 1941 France Libre commemorative stamp issues.

www.ingramcontent.com/pod-product-compliance
Lightning Source LLC
Chambersburg PA
CBHW042055290426
44111CB00001B/17